BIG JIMMY GILHEANEY
– MY STORY

BIG JIMMY GILHEANEY – MY STORY

The rise of the bone breakers

JIMMY GILHEANEY

Publishing by UK Book Publishing

www.ukbookpublishing.com

ISBN: 978-1-916572-58-4

CHAPTER 1

ALL BREEDS OF TRAVELLERS have their individual Clan names such as Fury or Gorman. My clan is called the Gilheaneys; we are a very proud family, our roots spread from Ireland to Scotland and literally all over the world, but the story of the Welsh Gilheaneys and how we got to Wales don't start with me or my brothers; in fact, it would have to start with my grandfather Jimmy. He was a quiet, respectable man but if you started him he could be very stubborn and hot tempered. I think he got that from the Heaneys because his old father Paddy Gilheaney was the quietest man in the world, pure harmless, but on the other hand his mother Bridgey was as game as a Yankee cock. I often heard the lads saying when she was insulted she would tie her hair up and have a fight with anyone; she was a gas woman anyway, she gave birth to my grandfather in the year 1928 in County Leitrim, northern Ireland, she reared him alongside her own people the Heaneys.

My grandfather Jimmy and my granny violet back in Ireland

I don't know much about the people today but back then the Heaneys were a well-respected bare-knuckle fighting family. As a matter of fact, my grandfather's uncle Pat was one of the roughest

1

men in northern Ireland; I hear he was a straight-talking man, who would take no messing off no one. During my grandfather's childhood, Pat Heaney was a big influence, he taught him respect and morals among other things. Anyway, when my grandfather became a man he met and married my granny Violet, and as a young couple they travelled up and down Ireland for years, but eventually they settled down in a little town called Lurgan which is located in County Armagh, Northern Ireland. Anyway, by the time my grandfather settled in Lurgan he had a total of 18 children, but having such a big family and considering it was made up of mostly wild young boys, understandably this brought a lot of worry to him, because in Ireland at the time the IRA was at their height and you wouldn't have to do a lot to get yourself into trouble. As a matter of fact my father actually witnessed one of his friends getting shot and killed right beside him, yeah Ireland was definitely a different place back then. I hear my grandfather would often lie in his bed at night and listen to gunfire and bombs going off – naturally it give him many a sleepless night about his family, but I think the final nail in the coffin that really got my grandfather worried, was when his youngest brother Willy was taken by three men with balaclavas on, they chucked him in the back of a van and brought him to a farmer's field. They tied him to a post and played Russian roulette with him, they pointed the gun at his forehead and pulled the trigger three times, click, click, click, but when they pointed the gun down at the ground and pulled the trigger it was then it went off, bang. My great-uncle Willy passed out with the fright. They later drove past my grandfather's house and chucked his brother Willy out of the van.

It was at that point my grandfather knew if he did not get his family out of Ireland he would be burying one of them, so he set down with my grandmother Violet and after talking it through they decided to move to Scotland where they could make a fresh start with their family. Well it turned out to be a good move because when my grandfather got to Scotland he opened up his own scrap yard, and him and his sons all worked in it together, well except for my father Willy because at the time he was a wild young man, he was fighting nearly every day; he was hot tempered and was getting into a lot of trouble. My grandfather tried to intervene, but my father was stubborn and he would not listen. Anyway one day he was outside of a chip shop and this Scottish lad come over and put his hand in my father's bag of chips – needless to say it was a very bad mistake for the Scottish lad to make. My father took to beat him within an inch of his life and when his hands were sore he started to beat him with a house brick – he nearly killed him. My father got locked up for that incident, he got three and a half years in jail.

While my father was serving his time, his brother Peter and Uncle Willy, my grandfather's brother, were travelling out of Scotland to England where Peter met and then married his wife Margaret. She was a Welsh woman so he later moved to Wales to start a family. My grandfather's brother Willy met Margaret's sister Jean and they also got married and moved to a place called Welshpool in North Wales.

Meanwhile, my father was serving his time in Scotland. As you can imagine, the jails back then were very rough and because my father had such a hot temper it meant that he had to fight nearly every day. This went on for some months, until one morning he was in the changing room and a fight started with him and another inmate. This man was a big unit, he stood six foot with an inch of hair all over his body; he and my father took to fight, it was shot for shot for about ten minutes, in a life or death fight. My father caught him a right hand into the mouth and blew the teeth out of his head – he often told me of the noise that the man's teeth made when they scattered across the marble floor. Needless to say, the man was left in a bad state; in truth, I think he must have been the cock of the jail because after that fight no one came to fight my father again. As he would walk out on the landings no one would even look him in the eye, they all held their heads down, which was a good thing.

Anyway, he served a little under two years, but after getting released he vowed to make a fresh start. At the time my grandfather was doing well with his scrap yard, but my father wanted to find his own path, and talking to family he heard his brother Peter had moved to Wales. He was close to Peter so he decided to follow on. My father came to Swansea in 1972 where he met my mother Mary Jones; she was a Romany gypsy girl from a quiet family. They hit it off straight away – as a matter of fact, I think it was love at first sight, because within two weeks of meeting her they were married. My father settled down

My mother and father on their wedding day

well in Swansea, he bought himself a six-cylinder Bedford TK lorry. My mother and father were very hard-working people. He used to cut cars up with a hatchet, he would cut the doors, roof and bonnet and sides off with the hatchet, and then by using a block and tackles he would load them on his lorry. The tackles had three 16-ft scaffold poles; it was a handy bit of kit. A funny thing happened with the block and tackle, well funny to us anyway. One day my father got a scrap lorry to move. He cut the cab up with the hatchet and then he lifted the chassis and engine with the poly blocks. He was telling my mother to reverse in the lorry, while he had the chassis and engine suspended in the air and she backed back too fast and hit one of the poles; it flipped around and hit my father on the backside. It left him black and blue he was effing and blinding for ten minutes straight. At this time my mother was in a kink laughing, but at the time my father never found it one bit funny. The pole had hit him that hard that it had bent. He had to straighten it up by putting it in the rim of the lorry – how bad of a smack did he ever get when it bent a scaffold pole! My father was a very tough man because to be honest I would have left the full lot, but he carried on loading the lorry and he got it on with my mother's help of course; it was good going without a Hiab. They were hard times but good times all the same. My mother never lived this down though, he still tells her about it to this day, jokingly of course; he always says she could have killed him, but my mother just laughs.

Anyway, there was another time that she almost got him jail; it was when my father got an old car to take away. This old car had no towing hitch so in order to tow it he had to put the chain on the engine mount. It was just to get it to the scrapyard, so as long as they took their time it would be fine. Anyway, my mother was towing him with the lorry while he was steering the old car, but on the way to the scrapyard they had to stop at a traffic lights and while they were stopped my father looked over at a policeman that was standing out of his car. The man never took no heed to them, he actually saluted my father and my father did the same back, but when my mother saw the policeman she panicked and took off hard, and as she did the engine ripped straight out of the car. She never looked back and as she was going along the road the engine was swinging on the chain back and forth. My father was panicking all shapes and the policeman was in shock. He walked over and gave my father a push with the shell of the car to get it off the road, then my father had to get in the police car and follow on after my mother because she never stopped. When he eventually caught up with her she said she never saw what happened. I could imagine the mood my father was in, but thank god the policeman never bothered – you see, back then you didn't even need a seatbelt; it would be a different case in this day and age. I don't think my father found it funny at the time, but it definitely was funny looking back.

Anyway, moving forward, Peter and my father were doing really well in Swansea and eventually word got back to my grandfather in Scotland, on how well they were doing and how nice the people were in Wales, so my grandfather decided to sell his scrap yard and to make the move himself to Wales. Naturally, most of the family followed. Meanwhile, as a young couple, my father and mother, and by this time much of the Gilheaney

Me as a baby and my mother

family, travelled up and down all of Swansea, camp to camp, but when my grandfather came down from Scotland he found a camp called the morganite. He was the first travelling man to open the gate; as the years went by though, the Gilheaneys wouldn't have Wales to themselves because every breed of an Irish traveller would come and go. As for me growing up in the 80s, it was great. It was a completely different way of life to what we have today – travellers at the time didn't have a lot, but what they did have they would share, even a strange traveller would bring you in with their own children and give you a plate of food and they wouldn't think nothing of it. At that time out of respect you would call everyone your uncle or aunt even though they were not your blood, it was just respect. Back then my father would be considered a wealthy man, he had a new 87 D reg Bedford TL lorry with a 650 Square boom push and pull Hiab on it; at the time it was the talk of Swansea, it was a fine lorry. As a bedroom he had a new Roma trailer for him and my mother and sisters. I remember it having blue plastic windows and for his kitchen trailer he had a buccaneer – it was where me and my brothers slept, it had cut glass windows and mirrors. If you had the same trailer today it would be worth a lot of money.

Anyway, back then a family pulled together as a unit, everyone had their chores. Every morning at 7 a.m. it was my job to light the stove. After I lit the fire I would go out and tidy up the yard, then after we got breakfast we would go to work and when we got home it was my job to start the generator. It was an old Lister Petter engine, I remember you needed a handle to start it but when I turned the handle it sometimes would kick back and sprain my wrist. Needless to say most of the time my wrist was sore. Come to think about it, I really hated that generator. Anyway, we never had constant electricity or flowing water, but I enjoyed it.

I remember as a boy getting up at 6:30 in the morning, the frost would be thick on the ground, I would have to break the ice in the churns to get to the water then pour it into a basin just so I could wash my face; it was very refreshing. Then I used to pour the water into the lid for a drink – you've never tasted nicer water, it was freezing cold, it was beautiful. Even the food was nicer. I remember my mother cooking dinner in a black pot outside on a fire, if it wasn't raining. This is how she would cook: she had the black pan for breakfast, she even had the black kettle – a cup of tea or a bacon sandwich cooked like that you've never tasted nothing like it. I think it must've been the smell of the wood burning or just the way the food was prepared, but either way once I was grown up food never tasted quite the same. There were a lot of good things growing up in the 80s but one bad thing I used to hate is when me and my brothers got really dirty, my mother would strip us to our underpants and put us in a big bath. I was always last to get in. I had to be dragged kicking and screaming. She would wash your hands and push the blood to the tip of your fingers and it would sting very bad, and I hated that, but we were always clean and well fed and well minded and you can't ask for no more than that.

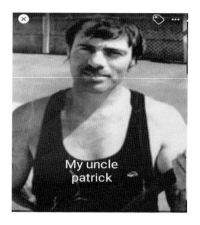

My uncle patrick

Anyway, moving forward, my father has a few close brothers but none closer than his brother Patrick. As I was growing up I became very close to my uncle Patrick. In his day he was a bloodthirsty man that could have a fight, but growing up I never heard a man say a wrong word about him, only that he was a gentleman. He was the kind of man if you give him respect you got respect. Growing

7

up, my uncle Patrick taught me a lot of things which I never forgot, he said it costs nothing to be nice and no matter how good of a man you become, nephew, never take a liberty. They were wise words but I later learnt you can't be nice to a donkey, as I would call them, because them kind of people see it as a weakness; don't get me wrong, you can be nice to nice people, you will get respect off them, but a donkey will try and beat you if you show any kind of weakness. You can always tell good people from the donkeys if you stand back and observe. Anyway my uncle Patrick had six children, five girls and one boy, but tragedy would strike his little family: his daughter Violet would die with brittle bone disease when she was only eight years old and his only son Patrick died of the same disease when he was just three months old. This brought a lot of heartache to my uncle Patrick, and if that wasn't bad enough one day he went working and while he was away his daughter Rosie was in the trailer sitting by the fireplace. Being a child, and not thinking, she threw a bottle of nail varnish into the fire and it exploded back on her, she caught a flame and panicked and ran outside. My father saw this and he ran over with an old carpet and wrapped her up in it. She was rushed to Chepstow hospital, and my uncle Patrick was contacted to make his way to the hospital. Rosie had severe burns on over 38% of her body. Patrick would be back and forward for months to the burns unit in Chepstow hospital. My uncle Patrick always had time for us; even though he was going through all that he still managed to keep a smile. It just shows you, you never know what's on someone's mind.

Anyway, growing up, I had some fun memories of my uncle Patrick. There was this one time some of our cousins moved down from Scotland. There was a boy, he was about 18, I could have been no more than 12 but he tried to bully me. He was saying how good of a martial artist he was. I laughed at him, I said, while I laughed, "you think you can fight?" – "yeah," he said. I smirked at him and said we will see. Later on I got him in front of my uncle Patrick, and being the little bastard I was, I said, "Uncle, he said he could beat you." Patrick laughed and said

"What?" So I said he was saying that he was the best martial artist in Swansea. My uncle Patrick laughed and said "right, get out here" to this 18 year old. Patrick jumped up and before touching the ground he hit him with two kicks on the side of the head. The boy was staggering all over the place. I laughed and said, "You're not so good now." My uncle Patrick winked at me and he said while he laughed, "You see, Jimmy, son, they're not so hard when you stand up to them." He knew the boy was a bully but even so, he still didn't hit the boy hard he just tapped him to put him in his place. The lesson I learnt from this is it's no good having a big mouth if you can't back it up, but I must admit it was pretty easy and funny getting Uncle Patrick to beat him up haha.

Moving forward, in 1988 my father, my uncle Peter and my grandfather put a petition in for the morganite to be turned into an official site. Within the year the council had built it, and we picked the biggest plot – my father needed the space because by this time he had nine children, six boys and three girls. After a few months on the site my father decided to give us a break so we pulled to Welshpool to my great-uncle Willy and my aunt Mary, which was great because growing up, Mary's son Steven and me were best friends, and that just made for a better holiday as every day me and Steven would go fishing and hunting and building dens and swings. It was all good fun, and looking back, great memories, but in fairness we all had good laughs in Welshpool. For instance, one week my great-uncle Willy was walking to the pub; he walked past a bridge and beneath it there was a flowing river. A week later he was walking back from the same pub drunk with my father and a couple of the boys, it was a very hot summer's night so to cool down he decided to jump in for a swim, but when he came to the bridge he never looked before he jumped and when he did jump the water had dried up and he fell onto the rocks and broke himself up. It was very funny at the time, well to us anyway. Poor old Willy wouldn't have thought so, he came home bruised and battered. My father laughed for an hour. Willy was a comical old man. We had a good summer that year but my father decided to get home, so we said our goodbyes and set off. On the way back to Swansea we pulled into a car park in Newtown. It was just outside Welshpool. We got settled and then at about 10 that night some people shot the side of my father's trailer with a gun. I remember lying in my bed and hearing the sound of

Me daddy willy Peter and tessa

the bullet hitting off the side of the trailer. At the time it was so scary, I remember I didn't get a lot of sleep that night. But the next morning we made our way back to Swansea and we quickly got back to normality.

A few months went by and my father met a man that introduced him to a fair called the Royal Welsh. We worked hard all summer so he thought it would be a nice break for the family, so on the 19th of July 1990 for the first time we shifted to Builth Wales. We were all having great fun until my sister Tessa decided to go swimming in the royal Welsh river, she got caught up in a whirlpool and she was drowning. I jumped in to save her and when I did she panicked and was pulling me under and drowning me as well. My father jumped in and grabbed the two of us, he chucked me one way and swam to the shore with Tessa. I doggy paddled back to the stones where I was exhausted. Another couple of minutes and me and my sister would have drowned. My father was a strong man to save us, we were very lucky. Anyway, on a bit happier note, the next day the family was having a picnic in the park beside the river, and me and my father started doing a bit of play fighting. There was this mesh that held in the rocks on the river bank. I was standing on it and my father lunged in to throw a right hand. I jumped to the side and he missed me; with his momentum he fell forward and his big toe got stuck in the mesh and he fell down the bank about 10-ft into stinging nettles. My mother and I were rolling around the ground laughing but my father did not find it funny. I had to stay out of his way for a good few hours. Eventually though, he did see the humour in it. The next morning his big toe was black and blue, it looked very sore. Looking back me and my father often had good laughs together and it all made for good memories and at the end of the day that is what life is all about.

Anyway, anyone that knows the Royal Welsh will tell you the field for the travellers is at least four miles out of the town, but back then the Field was right beside the town; as a matter of fact you had to drive through the town to get on or off the field. Thinking nothing of it, my father decided to go for a drive. It was about 4 pm in the afternoon and there was no one around. We didn't know it at the time because it was our first time being there, but Builth Wales town in the evening got very busy. My father had to drive his new van back through the town centre to get to the field but by this time there were hundreds of people standing out. While my father was driving, I remember being in the back of the van and there was a gang of men punching the side of the motor and trying to tip it over. I remember my father leaving a roar out of his body and saying to the men, "get down off the side of my motor or I'll kill everyone of youse". A man stepped out from the crowd – I think he must have been some kind of leader – he said, "get back, lads and leave the man get through". He looked at my

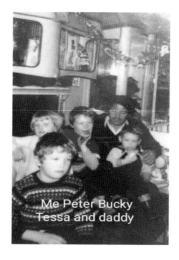

Me Peter Bucky Tessa and daddy

father and said, "I've never seen a pluckier man than you, why don't you join us for a drink?" My father said "that will do" to the man, then he dropped us back to the field and went down and drank with the men. All night he never put his hand in his pocket, they carried him all night. Me and my brothers and sisters lit a fire and started cooking spuds on sticks and telling ghost stories all night. I was trying to frighten Bucky, Mary and Michael and my sister Violet, but I think Peter, Willy and Tessa got more frightened than the children. We had a good time that year.

Tessa violet bucky Mary and Michael

Anyway, we came back to Swansea on the 28th of July, and on the 31st my uncle Patrick came knocking on my father's window. He asked my father was he going for a few beers, but he had just come back from the Royal Welsh so he said, "Patrick, I've had enough of the beer, you go on your own and I'll see you tomorrow." Patrick said, "OK, brother, see you tomorrow." Patrick went to the Crown pub in Morriston; he did his usual thing, couple of games of pool, few pints, and when he came out of the pub he walked into the Chinese to order some food. There was a man in there who kept staring at him. Patrick was a hot-tempered man so he said, "Who are you staring at, mate?" Without warning, the man made a punch for Patrick, Patrick went mental and hit the man four or five punches. The man runs out of the Chinese and Patrick chased him. The man did a u-turn and ran back into the Chinese and locked the door. Patrick was banging the door for him to come out and fight. By this time the police were called and when the police come to the scene they put my uncle Patrick to the ground and handcuffed him. They allegedly hit him with a truncheon on the back of the head which busted a blood vessel, and he was dead before he got to the hospital. He was only 36 years old. This devastated the Gilheaney family: my father went into a deep depression for years over this; I was 13 years old and I had lost a father figure, a man I had great respect for; the family would never be the same again. And as for the legal issues, there was nothing done to the police for their involvement and the man Patrick was arguing with – it was proved he started on Patrick and all he got was a £15 cost of courts and walked out a free man. Patrick never got no justice but it turns out the man that started the argument must have been a bastard because not long after this he was working in a mechanics yard and a couple of men walked in and beat him within an inch of his life and left him with a limpy leg – maybe a bit of karma, who knows. Anyway when my uncle Patrick died his wife Ann was five months pregnant, and when she did have the baby, at only three months old the child had a cot death. And if that was not bad enough, a couple of years after my uncle Patrick died his youngest little girl was out playing on the road and she was run over and killed by a car. He only has two surviving daughters today: Rosie and Margaret. His life truly was a tragedy for such a lovely person. If you took the time to read his headstone it would bring a tear to anyone's eye.

CHAPTER 2

ANYWAY, MOVING FORWARD, NOT long after my uncle Patrick's funeral, I was standing around with the boys and a fellow called Bill Cash. I think there's quite a few people that would like to give Bill a slap for this, but this is the truth – he comes over to me, he said, "Hi Jimmy, what are you doing for an hour or two?" I said, "Nothing, Bill, why?" He says, "Do you want to come down to the local boxing gym?" I thought about it; I was doing nothing else so I said, "yeah no problem I'll give it a go". The name of the gym was the Dockers Club, the coach's name was Mush Paddy. I walked in and did a couple of rounds on the bags and Mush Paddy walked over to me. "Alright, kid, have you boxed before?"

I said, "No sir."

He looked at me a bit funny but I was telling the truth; I had never boxed before. I think he was used to the little boys from the houses, but as a traveller boy growing up, fighting was commonplace. Nearly every day I went out to play I got a black eye or a busted mouth – I must have unknowingly learnt a little bit because he said, "You move well, you're a strong kid, would you spar one of the boys?"

I was all excited; I said, "No problem." I put the head guard on and got into the ring. For about a round the boy beat me up, I was all over the place but I managed to catch him by chance, a beautiful right hand and knocked him through the ropes.

Mush immediately said to me, "What's your name?"

I said, "Jimmy."

Me boxing

"Well done, Jimmy," he said. "You want to make a go of this? You've got something."

I said, "Thanks, sir, I will."

The truth was that I had found something that I really enjoyed and from then on I was hooked, I became very dedicated and as time went on I started to learn how to box and to throw straight punches, so Mush Paddy decided to put me in for my first fight. I had only been boxing a couple of months so I think he rushed me, but for two rounds I was beating the boy, I was too strong for him, but in the third round he caught me a punch smack on the nose but due to a lack of experience, when the blood was running out of my nose I touched it and the referee immediately stopped the fight. I wanted to carry on, I tried to argue my case, but the referee wasn't having none of it, he never gave me a chance. I always felt that he was a bit prejudiced but it was too late, I had lost my fight. This hit me hard so I vowed if I could help it I would never leave it to the judges or referees again. I fought a few more times for Mush Paddy and I knocked everyone I got in with out in one or two rounds. This got to the attention of a man called Mario Maccarinelli.

Mario met my father in a car boot sale and said to him, "Willy, I heard your son is very powerful. If you bring him to my gym I will teach him how to box." My father thought about this and decided to put me in the Bonymaen Boxing Club. I was 14 years old. You wouldn't get a better gym at the time, there was the likes of Rocky Reynolds, Nigel Page, Valo Maccarinelli and a good few more that would come in sparring and teaching little pro tricks; I felt

Me and Mario macronelli

Me and my daddy

right at home. Then you had Mario Maccarinelli, in my opinion the best trainer to ever come into Wales – my boxing and training was going very well.

Anyway, a few months later out of the blue, my father's youngest brother Sonny was standing out with a few of my cousins, he was trying to make a laugh off my boxing. He said to me, sniggering, "Put on the sparring gloves and we'll have a spar."

Now at the time Sonny was bullying all the young boys, but I was always a very bullheaded young man, so I said, "yeah no problem", and I put on the gloves. I actually schooled him, I could hit him at will, I think if I wanted to I could have cut the two eyes out of his head. He got enraged and started ripping his gloves off, so I said, "Let's have it." Sonny was 18 at the time and I was only 14, but I was game to fight. However, when my father looked over and had seen what was going on he went mental and tried to split us up. Sonny actually nearly caused an argument between my father and grandfather, but thank god before it got out of hand some of the family came out and stopped it. When everyone calmed down I was put in home and told to be quiet. Sonny got a bad shaman though he was embarrassed in front of his mates. At the time I thought nothing of it but this deeply hurt Sonny – he would hold this in his head for life. But the truth was he got arrogant and underestimated me, but what he didn't realise is when every other little boy was off playing snooker or enjoying themselves with some kind of activity, I was training. I would get up at six in the morning and put a 50 kilo rucksack on my back and run three miles before work. You see at the time in my mind to be the best you had to train harder than the rest, I believed that then and I believe that now, but when you get so fit it brings supreme confidence which is a good thing, but when it turns to arrogance like it did with Sonny it can be your undoing. Nevertheless, overconfidence can happen to anyone as I was about to learn because I was winning everything in my eyes I was unbeatable, but as the old saying goes, no matter how good you are you'll always run into your match. I was 15 years old, I was out in a boxing tournament in the Sandfields in Port Talbot, full of confidence, I went out to the sound track 'Another one bites the dust'; I had it played as my ring entrance song. The place was packed with travellers. I got in with this boy but at the time it never occurred to me that there were levels to boxing, something I was about to learn the hard way. The boy brought me into deep waters, he was one of the best boxers I ever boxed. I genuinely couldn't do nothing with him. I got frustrated and lost my temper, and in a moment of madness in the third round when the

Me boxing

referee tried to split us up, I hit him and knocked the referee out, but as soon as he hit the canvas my head cleared and I immediately regretted it. I tried to lift the man up and apologise but understandably he was having none of it. Afterwards I felt sorry for the boy that I was boxing but the look of terror on his face as he ran back to his corner was priceless. In all fairness though, he was beating me, but if it was any consolation to the boy I had a two-year ban from boxing and at the time that was worse than the beating.

After this incident there were two things I had to do: I had to try and learn to control my temper and try to be humble. Anyway, moving forward, later on that year we went travelling to England, me and my father done gardening work, cutting down trees, landscaping, laying patios. We worked hard all summer. I remember this one job where we had to completely landscape the woman's garden. As we were moving some brambles and some rusty old bins, no exaggerating there must have been 100 snakes! After seeing that I was on tenterhooks for the whole job, I have a bad phobia of snakes, I hate them, but needless to say we did a very good job; we put in pathways, planted shrubs and put in a rockery for the woman and after all that work and fright over the snakes, she cheated us out of our money. My father went mental but what could we do? I wanted to smash up the garden, but my father wouldn't let me. I suppose some you win some you lose.

Anyway while we were out travelling, we stopped off at a Christian convention in Nottingham where my uncle Moshi on my mother's side was stopped. The field he was on was massive – I'll bet there were 3000 trailers on there. Me and my father and a few of the boys stood watching a fight. There was this big man and a skinny man, they took to fight. I said to my father "the little man is gonna get knocked out", but he said "not necessarily, son", and no sooner did he say it, when the little man bit the big man's ear off, the big man quit and walked off holding the side of his head. I remember the blood was pouring through his fingers. As a result of this a load of trouble kicked off on the field – there were cars rammed, trailers shot, people cut up; they started

Me the day of my holy communion

speeding past my father's place, my father went mental and roared up the full field, he said, "I'll kill every man on the ground" – ok he might have been exaggerating a little bit because there was an awful big gang of men standing around, but my father is not a man to bluff, he would have a fight in a second, and the men must have known this because not one stepped out for a fight. Anyway, after they all walked away, my father went in home. When we got up the next morning the field was nearly empty, they had left early hours of the morning. After a few days we made our way back to Swansea to homebase. We had a good summer that year, some laughs, some shocks, but that's just some of the highs and lows of the travelling life.

When I got back to Swansea, I started working on my own. I was only 16 years old, but back then we never bothered with such things as a driving licences – yes, you could actually drive without a licence, not legally of course, but back then you could get away with it; you couldn't do it today though.

Anyway, I was driving every day, working away, but one day I finished work early and I was relaxing in my trailer watching a bit of telly. My friend Miley Cash came to me and said, "Jimmy, are you coming off with the boys to try and get a couple of girls?"

I said, "yes, Miley, wait till I get dressed," and I was ready in minutes. I jumped in the car with Miley and the boys and off we went to Birchgrove. I got a couple of girls and I was chatting to them, then this Connors man come to the car and tried to chat over me to the girls, which I found very ignorant. You see, at the time this fellow was 23 years old, so he looked at me as a bit of a boy – that was his first and last mistake. He tried to pull his bluff, so I said, "stop your carrying on or I'll split your two eyes", one word bore the other and a fight was on. We were in a housing estate so I said "follow me back up to the golf course and we'll have a few bangs". I drove back up and jumped out of the car. Miley Cash showed fair play for the two of us and although I was young I was a well-established boxer, but as I would learn: ring fighting and bare knuckle is completely different. The way I see it, bare-knuckle is like jogging on the roads and mountains, and ring fighting is like running on a running machine – it looks the same but there is a big difference, and because I was not used to fighting outside we fought for about 45 minutes, which in my opinion is no brag because a good fight shouldn't last no more than 15 or 20 minutes. In all honesty if I was in the ring I would have knocked this fellow out in one round, but on the cobbles he could keep running back and out of range. I struggled a bit to find my distance but when I did I started hitting him at will;

I dropped him five times and I broke him up, he was left with the blood running out of him. The next day I learnt that this man was one of the best of his name, which made me feel a bit better because I was a bit disappointed in the length the fight went, but regardless of what I thought, it was a very good win. Two days after the fight my father's youngest brother Sonny asked me about the fight; he said, "You didn't beat Paddy Connors, did you, he's a rough old chap?"

I knew he was trying to be smart so I said, "I did beat him, Sonny, and it was easy work and what of it?"

He smirked at me and walked off. A few days later he made it his business to get me and the man in the same car and he asked him in front of me. The man told Sonny that I beat him in the best of fair play and that I was a very tough boy. This was like slapping Sonny in the face, you could see he was upset; it was as if he wanted me to lose. Looking back now, I know he did, but at the time being young and stupid I never took no notice of him. But one good thing me and Paddy Connors through the years we became very good friends.

CHAPTER 3

ANYWAY MOVING FORWARD, THE next year we went to the Royal Welsh. My brother Willy was going strong with a girl called, ii, she had a cousin called Bridget; ii came to visit Willy on the field and Bridget and a couple of other girls came for a spin with her. I was in the Builth Wales Town with a couple of the boys and after an hour or so I decided to drive back to the field. I got out of my car and I walked to my father's place and there she was, sitting on the grass, Bridget. She had a black bandana on her forehead and long blonde hair. I was spell bound, I could not stop staring at her; she was beautiful. At the first chance I got I asked her out on a date and she thankfully accepted. When I got back to Swansea we were going steady. There was a place I brought her one night in Gorseinon called the Lovers Lanes. We were sitting chatting, listening to music; it was pitch black, you couldn't see your hand in front of your face. Bridget looked up into the trees and she could see the butt of a fag sucking in the darkness. She showed it to me and I thought it was a devil or something – I panicked and put the pedal to the metal, I nearly broke up the motor I went that fast out of those lanes and I never went back there again. At the time I got a bad fright and I gave Bridget a bigger fright with the carry-on out of me, but I later realised it was only some pervert smoking a fag, staring at us anyway. Within five months I had asked her to marry me. She actually said no, my face went red and I was just going to chuck her out of my motor lol, but before I could do anything she started laughing at me, and said I'm only playing, of course I will marry you. I was very happy and relieved, but now due to respect I had to go to England to ask her father for her hand. You see at the time Bridget was staying with her aunt and uncle in Swansea, so it meant I had to pick her up early in the morning and drive through to Luton to her father and mother's place. Anyway, her father's name was Wacker Harty, I knew of him because years beforehand he used to stay in Swansea and during that time I became good mates with his sons Ozzy and Parr, but even so I was still ashamed but I had no choice. I pulled back my two shoulders, took a deep breath and, I went into the house and sat on the settee. There were loads of young children around me and every one of them had red hair. I remember I was sitting there smiling, thinking to myself I hope Bridget's not red headed, please let her be natural blonde, and then all of a sudden Wacker comes down the stairs and sat staring at me. I was very ashamed but I said, "Well, sir, I've come to ask for your daughter's hand in marriage." Surprisingly to me he never hesitated, he said, "Yes, son, no problem, when do you want to marry her?" I looked up nervously and I said, "as soon as possible", he said, "ok leave it with me". I thought, that went alright, so I said "thank you, sir" and walked out of the house. Outside I met a couple of Bridget's brothers, one in particular, Thomas; we hit it off straight away, he was a nice fella. We went off for a drive in his cabstar pickup,

Me and my
brother-in-law Thomas

he was having a bit of sport so he took me from one side of Luton to the other side in minutes. He was laughing, speeding like a madman; on a couple of occasions he nearly got me killed out of the pickup. I was telling him to slow down but all he could do was laugh; I think he was showing off his driving, but as far as I was concerned he was just a bad driver. One thing for sure I was very glad to get back to the house

– when I got out of the motor I nearly kissed the ground, but I knew I had to let on it didn't bother me so I let on to laugh it off but I remember thinking I won't be getting in with you again lol. Anyway, apart from Thomas' driving skills, I thought they were nice people, so I headed back to Swansea and yes on the way back I did crack a joke and asked Bridget about her hair colour – she just looked at me and laughed. I said ok then as I stared at the road ahead of me, imagining my kids with red hair, haha only joking. Anyway, I dropped Bridget

Me and my wife Bridget on the day of our wedding

back off to her aunt and uncle, but little did I know that Wacker and his wife would come that night and take Bridget out of the house – because the Gilheaneys had a rough name they thought their daughter was going to be in a bad marriage. But my Bridget told them straight: "If you

don't let me marry him, I will run off with him." She gave them no choice so her father arranged the wedding and we got married. The night of my wedding everything was going well until Sonny showed up; he started bullying and causing mischief. I was enjoying myself and that night I don't remember seeing much of Sonny, but after I had left the wedding I think he hit a couple of old harmless people. Anyway, the next day I moved to England, but while I was gone my father went and pulled Sonny about carrying on at his son's wedding, but when he did, Sonny had a chip on his shoulder and got cheeky to my father, so my father told him, "less your cheek, Sonny". Sonny actually tried to make a punch for him, my father let a couple of punches go back at Sonny but my grandfather intervened between them. There was a bit of a persuading match between my father and my grandfather, but in all fairness Sonny was out of order. My father was a man with a big family of children, Sonny was only 21 years old; the truth is he tried his luck and when he realised my father was too strong for him he pulled in his horns. Anyway, Sonny would later try his luck down the line but that's a story for later.

Anyway, I was doing well in Yorkshire with my brother-in-law Willy Boswell. We were buying and selling a few motors together, but one day Willy got in this little petrol transit van, it was a 1990 on a G-reg so I had a bit of dealing with him and bought the van. The boys were advising me to convert it from petrol to diesel because this would add more money to the van, but I'd never done it before and as a result when I installed a diesel engine, the van was pulling back and air locking, so I fixed a couple of bits and I took it for a test drive. I remember the snow was thick on the ground, the van was still pulling back badly, but being young and foolish I drove the van about 15 miles from the site and the van broke down. I was stuck on the side of the road. My wife Bridget had to sit in the van while I walked on to try and get some diesel. I managed to get some off a lorry driver; he had a 2-litre Coke bottle and he filled it up with diesel for me. I couldn't thank the man enough, I was walking back along the road when it started to blizzard; I could barely see where I was going. Being from Swansea I'd never seen snow like it in my life. When I got back I had to climb beneath the van and disconnect the two pipes from the diesel tank. There was a stream of ice cold water running on the road that I was lying in, it went straight through my back; I was never as cold in my life. I took the two pipes and pulled them back up beside the engine, I put the pipes directly into the bottle inflow and outflow – I had seen my father do it before – and thank god it worked and got me back to the site. The next morning my wife Bridget wanted to go travelling so I fixed the van the best way I could and said thank you to Willy for all the hospitality

24

Me and my
brother-in-law parr

and I went travelling with my brother-in-law Thomas Mike Qulligan and my brother-in-law Parr; we were all young people trying to earn money and have a laugh; they were good times.

Anyway I remember once we were shifting to a different camp, my brother-in-law Thomas had a transit van and a Tabbert trailer he was showing off, trying to race his brother, Parr, and he got into a speed wobble; the trailer and van were going from one side of a dual carriageway to the other – how he got back control I'll never know. He wasn't as bad a driver as I first thought, he was just heavy footed. True, Thomas's speeding and my van not going too well, we somehow got to the new camp in Northampton, I settled my trailer and then I decided to go to London to visit my brother-in-law Ozzy and to see my uncle Moshi, but my van wasn't going too well so I left it on the camp and lent my brother-in-law, Parr's car, but when I got to London it was a busy city that I was not used to. After a couple of days or so I crashed the front of Parr's car; I panicked a bit and drove straight to the site and I tried to fix the car at Ozzy's place but I hadn't seen Ozzy since I was a boy and all he wanted to do was chat. He wouldn't sit down for a second, he walked me up and down the whole of London, my legs were killing me and I was super fit at the time so it will tell you how much walking he did. He meant no harm, he was just trying to be homely, but if it was today he could walk by himself – I would have stayed in the trailer with a cup of coffee – but that's a part of being young and foolish. Anyway, I left London and made my way back to the camp in Northampton, I parked the car facing in the way so Parr couldn't see it, at this time he had my van fixed perfect so the van drove like new. I felt a bit guilty about Parr's car as I was hooking my trailer on to leave, but I kept my mouth shut.

Thankfully I didn't see Parr for a couple of years but eventually after a lot of nagging from him I did pay him for his car.

Anyway, I was a few months gone so I decided to get back home to Swansea. On the way back down I got to the Bristol bridge but I had barely any diesel in, and I had my trailer hooked to the back of my van and I had no money in my pocket. I didn't know at the time you had to pay to cross the bridge, so I couldn't go past, I couldn't turn back because I didn't have any diesel. I remembered I had a small few pounds in the bank but it was about six at night. Needless to say it was a very long evening, me and my wife had to go to bed that night hungry. Anyway, the next morning I had to chance the van to the bank whilst towing my trailer, but thank god I managed to get a small bit of money though by this time the van was literally on fumes. Anyway, somehow I got to the garage, I put some diesel in and got some sandwiches. I'm not just saying it but they were the nicest sandwiches I ever tasted. After that night I always had a different respect for money, I would probably hit hard times after it, but I always had a value for money because of this night.

Anyway, moving forward, when I got back to Swansea I heard about the argument with my father and Sonny, over his troublemaking at my wedding. I said, "Father, you should have got in touch with me and chucked me out to him." He said, "Not to worry, son, I put him in his place." I said, "Fair enough." After that conversation I took a few months to myself. Being newly married I needed to earn money in a bad way, but when I stabilized myself, I decided to get back into boxing. As I was getting back into training a man called Nigel Page, a well-known and well-respected boxer in Swansea – I trained with Pagey before when I first went to the Bonymaen boxing gym so I knew him well – he came and asked me, he said, "do you

Me and my daddy doing the kilve hill cement run

want to take part in a charity event" that he was putting together – it would later be known as the Kilvey Hill Cement Run in Bonymaen. I said, "Of course I will, Pagey, what does it involve?" He said, "We all grab a 50 kilo bag of cement, put it on our shoulder and run up the mountain one mile with it, and then me and you, Jimmy, will put on a bit of a show, we will do a charity sparring match." I said, "That sounds good, Pagey, I'll have a go." A soldier won the race, Pagey came second, my father came third and I came fourth. Afterwards there was an outside open-air ring that was set up, there were people eating slugs for charity, all good fun. Me and Pagey got dressed up in our boxing gear and got in the ring. We started off the first couple of rounds going easy on one another, but we got carried away at certain points and it kind of turned into a bit of a fight. We'd done nine rounds when the referee stopped it and called it a draw; we earned over £2,000 that day for charity. Pagey was a very good friend; he would later lose his life by falling through a roof – he was only a young man but he is a Swansea legend and legends never die.

Anyway, I had a few more fights in the ring, I won them all, but any fighter will tell you that it's hard to keep disciplined when you're trying to earn a living. At this point I was a couple of years married, I had two sons, Willy and Thomas, and because of that I had to put work ahead of boxing so I decided to move to Yorkshire. My brother-in-law Willy Boswell was doing a bit and he asked me to move up with him, but as I was getting things ready to shift, my mother came running to me and said one of my brothers was arguing with a travelling man in the snooker club and the man had pulled a Stanley knife and tried to cut him. My blood boiled. I shouted over to my wife, I said to her, "I'll be back in 20-minutes." She was left packing the things down to shift. Anyway I left her to it and I jumped in my car and flew up to the snooker hall. When I walked in the man was standing there. I said, "Pull your Stanley knife out now and let's see what you're made of." He started shouting so I made a run towards him, he backed back but when I looked he had a Budweiser bottle in his right hand; he broke it off the table and made a stabbing action towards me. I stepped back and picked a snooker ball up and threw it at him, it hit him on the forehead and a lump came out as big as an egg. He was staggering all over the place. I stepped in and hit him a left hook and drove him under the snooker table; he was left unconscious. I told his mates who were with him, I said, "When he wakes up you tell him if he ever insults my family again I'll break every bone in his face." They all held their heads down because when you put bullies in their place, that's what they do. Truthfully, I've never seen men with more fear in their eyes. I laughed because a few minutes beforehand they were all killers, threatening to chop everybody up, but by knockin' their hero out it made them humble, lol.

Anyway I left it a day or so before I moved to Yorkshire. I didn't want the donkeys thinking I left because of them. Anyway when I got to Wakefield Willy asked me, "Why did it take you so long to get here?" I explained to him what had happened and he busted out

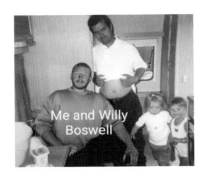

Me and Willy Boswell

laughing. He said, "You actually hit a man on the head with a snooker ball, god that must have been sore." I thought nothing of it when I did it, but Willy was right in what he was saying, because I'd say the poor old donkey did have a very sore head the next morning, haha. Anyway, moving forward, me and Willy got on very well. Willy and his family was very homely people, his old father Alfie Boswell was a comical old man, he would joke about anything. One day I was fixing an engine on Willy's plot when old Alfie walked over laughing and said, "Well, Jimmy son, did you fix the generator?" I said "yeah", and he looked up and said, "now you're sucking the diesel". I busted out laughing, I didn't mean to be ignorant to the old man, but I found it very funny. When I said it back in Swansea to the boys it was a standing joke from thereon in – for years anytime someone did something good we would look up and say, now you're sucking the diesel; it was pretty funny at the time.

Anyway, Willy's old mother Phyllis was a real homely old woman, she would constantly be trying to feed everyone. Me and Willy had done very well together buying and selling old motors, putting recovery trucks together, we even dabbled a bit in old trailers and campers; it was a very good living in them. But Willy was the brains, I was a worker and into metals and scrap. For some reason I could never get the swing of buying and selling motors, so I shook his hand and told Willy thanks for everything and I decided to move to Nottingham to my brother-in-law Thomas. Me and Thomas became very good friends, we would do uPVC fascias and tarmacking drives. I remember this one job we got we had to change all the downpipes, gutterings and fascias on a house, we brought in my brother-in-law Parr, he was a great man to do a job. I remember it was a beautiful summer's day, me and Thomas were in the back garden lying on the grass; we were drinking a couple of glasses of freezing cold lemonade, while poor old Parr was on the job with the sweat running out of him. Thomas started making a laugh of Parr, he was saying that Parr was a handy old boy to do a job. Thomas was having a joke like brothers do, but I got ashamed and tried to pass Parr materials. Meanwhile, Thomas was still laughing and relaxing on the grass when all of a sudden Parr started throwing bits of plastic at him. It was a good laugh but with the carry on out of the two of them I definitely thought we were getting locked up off the job – but thank God everything went well and we had a very good day; there was no evil or spite, just a laugh and a joke.

But as good a time as I was having with the boys, home is where the heart is, so I decided to go back to Swansea to homebase. However, as soon as I got back everyone was hooked up and ready to go to the Royal Welsh, so I didn't even hook off my trailer, I just followed on with the crowd. When we all got there I was surprised to see that Willy Boswell had shifted down to the Royal Welsh, which just made it a better crack.

Anyway, some years earlier my father started off a challenge to run up the mountain opposite the travellers' field, and every year after we'd done it as a family tradition, but soon enough all the travellers had a go. It's only a two-mile run but it's proper terrain, rivers, hedges bushes, it's good endurance; at some points you've got to get on your hands and knees to do it. I was the record holder that year, I'd done it in just over 17 minutes. My father had beaten me the year before so it was nice to get revenge, but in fairness to my father he did do it twice on the same day: he did it with Paddy Doherty at seven in the morning and later on in the afternoon he did it with big Danni Smith. It was all good fun, anyway. Later that night we were all hit with a torrential rain storm, no exaggeration, there was a foot and a half of muck, everyone was getting stuck all over the field except for my brother Peter and Willy Boswell. Willy had a Hilux pickup that had the big chunky tyres on it and Peter had a Sierra Sapphire. I could see into Willy not getting stuck but I don't know how Peter was getting away, he was just gliding in and out. We were all laughing because there were four wheel drives all over the field getting stuck left, right and centre, and the Sierra Sapphire was driving out past them. People were coming to Willy Boswell every few seconds for a tow, but eventually he had to pull every one of us off the field because the women had had enough of all the muck, though all the boys enjoyed it, and me and Willy had some sport in his Hilux pickup. However, when we got home it took a bit of doing for everyone to clean their trailers and motors, they were destroyed in muck.

Anyway, after a few days of being home Bridget wanted to go to London for the weekend to visit her brother Ozzy. As she was asking me all I could think about is what he put me through the last time I visited him, but he was a nice fellow so I said "let's go", and sure enough when I got to London he asked me to go for a drive with him. He drove me to every back lane in England. I said, "Ozzy, what are we doing out here in the sticks?" I didn't know it at the time, but he was bad with his nerves; he couldn't sit down for a second. I was glad to get back to his house. I tried to have an early night because I was tired all day running, but when I was asleep I was woken up by the smell of smoke and when I opened my eyes Ozzy's two children had lit a set of curtains on fire, it was ablaze. I jumped up, not thinking and grabbed them with my bare hands. My hands stuck to the curtains; I was badly burnt, but I managed to put them out. Later on that morning I said thanks for everything to Ozzy and I made my way back to Swansea. For the full journey I had to hold my hands out the window of the motor for the wind to cool the burns. Anyway, the next day me and my father were sitting out chatting, he was giving me a lecture for burning my hands, I was laughing and agreeing with him and then a car with four young lads drove in by my father's place, they were calling names out of the window. I ran over to give them a beating, but they put their foot down; they went about 100 yards and then stopped. I ran after the car and then the boys started making a laugh, every time I would try to run after them they would take off; but what they didn't know was that the boys on the site were getting tooled up and were about to pick me up. When the boys got me, we chased them all the way around the block; the young lads were panicking and crying and they made a mistake, because back then the dual carriageway by the site was just getting built, and what they didn't realise is when they drove on it, it was a dead end road and they had no choice but to come back on themselves. Now what I did next was very stupid: the boys stopped the car and I got out with a pick handle and stood in the middle of the dual carriageway while the panicking boys drove at me at a good 60 miles per hour. I stood my ground and as they came towards me I swung the pick handle and hit the windscreen. The glass blew all over them, and I nearly broke my burnt hands, the flesh fell off them, and I was nearly run over. Afterwards all the lads were saying that I was a madman to do what I had done, but it was just because I got that angry, I couldn't think straight. In fairness, looking back, it was very stupid, but my god they made my blood boil. Anyway, after this my hands had to be bandaged up and were sore for weeks.

CHAPTER 4

MOVING FORWARD, IN 1999 things got interesting. There was an empty plot beside me on the site and one day my father walked down and he said that his brother Sonny wants to pull onto the empty plot.

I said, "Daddy, it's up to you, he's your brother, but you know what he's like, he could start an argument in a nunnery."

My father smiled and said, "Give him a chance, son."

"Ok," I said, "no problem."

Sonny moved onto the plot, but there was no electric in his shed, so he asked me was it ok if he plugged into my shed. I said, "No problem, Sonny, carry on." First of all he seemed ok, he had lost a lot of weight due to a thyroid problem he had, but for a change we were getting on ok, until one day I was sitting watching my telly and my electric kept knocking off. I looked out my window and I saw Sonny jumping my fence and he plugged out my electric lead and chucked it across my plot. I thought what a cheeky thing to do, so I walked out and jumped the fence and said, "What are you doing, Sonny, why did you pull my lead out?"

He said, "Shut up or I'll knock you out."

I started laughing; he looked like he was going to die. I drew back and hit him two punches, he slapped off the side of his trailer, he fell to the ground and said, "wait, I'm too weak, I need time to train".

I said, "You look like you're going to die, get off the drugs."

My father ran down and split us up. He said, "Don't hit him, Jimmy, he's too weak." It was still his youngest brother, so I said, "He pulled my lead out, Father, and tried to make a fool of me and then he told me that he would knock me out."

My father laughed and said, "Son, how would he knock you out?"

I said, "You're right, Father," and I put Sonny off the site; I hate someone looking for trouble all the time so he got up and left. The truth is he had seen my kindness as weakness and he also had it in his head from the time we sparred when I was only 14. Anyway, Sonny went away that day and no one heard of him for a while. A week or two later I met my cousin Steven, my aunt Mary's son, in Blockbuster video shop, and he told me that Sonny was training for me. I laughed and said Sonny was only a fool. Anyway later that year I boxed for the senior light heavyweight Welsh title, and I won the fight by a unanimous decision. My brother Michael boxed the same night and Michael won his fight in the second round by a knockout. He would go on to do a lot more in the boxing ring, but this was my last ring fight; I was 22 years old. In my time I had a couple of Welsh school boy championships under my belt, but my favourite win in the ring was the senior Welsh title. Anyway my record stood at 28 fights, one loss and one disqualification, 26 wins. Mario Maccarinelli wanted me to go professional. I wanted to, but my father didn't want it – at the time he said travellers didn't do such things, he was just old fashioned. Mario even stopped talking to me because I didn't turn Pro, but eventually we would reconcile our differences. Anyway, by the end of 1999 my wife was heavily pregnant with our daughter Thoots, she decided that she wanted to be with her sisters and mother to have the baby, so I moved to Castleford, Yorkshire where I got a house and was working every day with my brother-in-law Thomas. I remember this one night I decided to go and get a takeaway, so I said to Thomas and his wife if they babysat my two boys we would go and get the food. They were OK with that so me and Bridget went to Castleford town. I got out of my car and walked over to the cashpoint to get some money; as I was walking back to my car four men were walking behind me. The biggest lad shouted out that he was the best man in Castleford.

I stopped and turned on my heel. I said, "Not while I'm here." It was a bit stupid looking back when I think about it, but anyway I ran straight over and punched the biggest man straight on the side of the head and dropped him. One of the other men came behind me and hit me with a Budweiser bottle on top of the head. I spun around and connected him a right-hand and dropped him. At this time the biggest man got back up, I backed up to look for a weapon, but the only thing I could see was a house brick, so I picked it up and as the big man ran in, I hit him straight on the side of the head with it; he never got up no more. My heavily pregnant wife was sitting in the car panicking, so I tried to back up, and then one of the men ran towards me, so I stepped to the side and the fool runs straight into a shop window. I spun towards him and I hit him a sharp one-two, he was flattened, then I jumped into my car and got out of there and headed back to my house. I was covered in blood, where my head was split open. Afterwards, Thomas laughed at me for being so stupid, and after all that I still never got the takeaway, lol.

Anyway on the 14th of November my wife had our daughter Thoots, thank God mother and baby was perfect. A few days after my daughter was born I bought myself a little pick up and I was working very hard, everything was going great and then I got bad news: an old friend of mine in Swansea called Davy Grey suddenly died, he was only 50 years old. Davy used to come down every morning to me for a cup of tea, we often had conversations that would last for hours, we'd become very good friends. I would take a lot of advice from Davy on arguments and fights that were happening in my life, he would always advise me for my best, I trusted his opinion. One thing he told me always sticks in my mind, you see I was always very keen to earn a living, always trying to come up with a new way of earning money, like most men – but one morning I was heading out to work and Davy looked at me and he said, "you know something, Jimmy, money is not everything". I laughed at him and said, "But it helps, Davy." Out of the blue he looked up and said, "You're never a poor man until you're in poor health." I laughed at the time, but he was right in what he was saying because after this happened to Davy I'm not sure what it was or how it happened, maybe it was the shock, I don't know, but something triggered in my mind. It started off slowly, I was just paranoid at first but it soon snowballed and after a few weeks I started to feel very down; I had no interest in anything; it made me very aware of my mortality. Maybe it was the shock of someone I knew very well to die so suddenly, I don't know. Either way it was the start of a very bad period in my personal life and then on top of all that out of the blue my mother rang me, and said, "Son, we was in the pub last night and Sonny started on your father."

My father was more than a match for Sonny, but before they could fight the family in the pub split them up. Sonny had it in his head for my father and thought because he was getting on a bit he would try his luck. I was feeling low, but I had to step up for my father so I phoned Sonny. I said, "What is your problem, Sonny, why are you trying to fight an old man?"

He said, "Do you know who you're talking to?"

I said, "I don't care who you think you are, you insult my father again and I'll put you in hospital." At this point I had had enough of Sonny, one word would bear the other and I told him straight: "Get your ass out today or tomorrow and we will have a fight."

He said, "No, I need time to train."

So I said, "How long do you need?"

He said, "At least three months."

I said, "Sonny, I heard you was training months ago, why do you need three months? Let's have it tomorrow."

He said, "I haven't been training, I've been on the bear."

So I said, "Ok, you got your three months." This was in April, so I said, "Sonny, we will fight on the 31st of July, my uncle Patrick's blessing."

He agreed, the fight was on and I couldn't wait. I would do some of my training in Yorkshire, but I was going through some funny emotions. At the time I didn't know nothing about depression and how it can suddenly get a hold to you, but regardless, I had a job to do. Anyway in Castleford there was a fireman living next door to me, we used to go jogging at five in the mornings, we would do 10 miles, three times a week. He was a very fit man but you need more than just jogging to fight, so I decided to move back to Swansea where my father would train me and I could get some good sparring in the Bonymaen gym. So when I came back to Swansea I went to Mario's house and I explained to him what was going on. Now I think he was still a little bit upset with me for not going Pro, but fair play to him he put that aside and told me I could have as much sparring as I needed. I said, "Thanks, Mario, I appreciate that." Anyway, training went very well and I was feeling very confident.

Now as I've mentioned the fight was scheduled for the 31st, but Sonny tried to pull a fly one, he came to the site on the 27th, now I believe it was in the hopes that he would catch me offguard, but thank God I was bouncing and ready. Now the last time I'd seen Sonny was when I hit him a couple of shots over an electric lead, and at that time he was about 14 stone, soaking wet, but when he came down to the site that morning he was clearly on steroids, he was about 18 stone, but it was nothing to me. I jumped straight out, my grandfather and a few of my uncles and cousins came with Sonny to show him fair play, my father showed me fair play. Now I've beat Sonny a good few times in sparring sessions over the years in the gym and out on the site, so as a fighter I did not have much respect for him. I know at the time he had a bit of a reputation, but I didn't rate him. The truth is I think I did underestimate him a bit, and maybe I didn't train the way I should have or it could have been the personal demons I was fighting in my mind; I'm not sure what it was, but either way the fight lasted for 35 minutes. I won't lie: on the day we had a good fight, it was shot for shot, I dropped him a couple of times; we even at one point dropped each other. He threw a right-hand and I threw a left hand and at the same time we dropped one another. In truth it was a good fight, the ground was painted red with blood, my grandfather and father were begging us to stop fighting, but I would not give best, I was prepared to die and to be fair, Sonny would not give best either. It was a very vicious fight: I cut the two eyes out of his head and split him to pieces, his eyes started to close up and he could not see where he was going. After about 25 minutes I was in full control of the fight. At one point he asked one of his brothers to slice his eyes to relieve the swelling, but it was no good, he had no choice but to quit. He had the cheek to say that he wanted to stop the fight on that day and continue the same fight on a different day, but I said "can you fight on, Sonny, yes or no?" – "no," he said. "Well," I said, "if you can't continue today you are beat."

He said, "We'll fight again."

I said, "No problem, when you heal, my grandfather and father will arrange a fight, but today you are beat." To say Sonny is a sore loser is an understatement, but he had no alternative, he had to take the loss. He was escorted to his Jeep where he was put in the back and brought to the hospital. He was released the same afternoon but after a few days he got infections in his eyes and as a result he could not see, so he had to be hand led to the toilet for a good two weeks, or maybe he just shit in a bucket lol. Either way he had sustained a hell of a beating. After the fight everyone was patting me on the back, but I had no interest. Months would go by and I deteriorated badly because depression is a terrible thing, especially when you don't even know what it is. It really got a hold to me, I was months not even coming out of my home; my wife didn't know what to do with me. I couldn't explain to her what was wrong because I didn't know myself, it was an awful thing to go through. In the night when I would go to bed and lock my door, I would have to get up all night and keep checking it because my mind kept telling me it wasn't locked. Even stupid little things like seeing the radio on an odd number, it would drive me mad, everything had to be level and just right. I remember one time I was sitting and I started scratching my arm, I lost track of time and when I came back to myself I realised that the blood was running out of me – I had scratched it that much that I split the skin. No doubt about it, my head was gone.

Anyway, a few days later my wife tried to cheer me up. She said, "Let's go to the pub with all the lads." I really didn't want to go but I felt sorry for her, so I said "ok". When I got there everyone was laughing and having a good time, so I tried to mingle. I sat down on a chair and I got overwhelmed with emotion; it's hard to explain but everything hit me all at once and I busted out crying. I was in a hell of a state so I left the pub with my wife. I remember I was walking home, sobbing like a child. I was an emotional wreck. As I was walking I remember coming to a bridge and for a split second I was going to jump off and kill myself, but as I grabbed the railings to jump, my wife grabbed me and dragged me to the ground. She said, "What are you doing, you fool?" I was on my knees crying. My wife picked me up and brought me home. You see, suicide had crossed my mind on a few occasions; but there's no doubt about it, only for my wife being there that night I would not be here to talk about it, so anyone who is thinking of such a thing, don't do it, because no matter how dark the night gets the sun will always rise. In my case I am so grateful to my wife for saving me. Anyway, getting back to my story, what had happened in the pub and on the way home it terrified my wife, so she said to me, "you've got to get up and shake yourself, you're only a young man and we've got three small children". The truth is at the time I had no interest in what she was saying so I caused an argument, but behind every good man there's a good woman. She stood her ground and made me get up and get out of the trailer. My wife had to drive me out working and for a travelling man there's nothing as shameful as that, but no matter who you are or how hard you are, sometimes everyone needs a push, or in my case a kick up the backside, lol. But all jokes aside, I really was in a bad place. I remember I had a crew cab transit pickup with three infants and nowhere to turn but my wife, god help her, was trying her best to help me. She found a yard full of big square Ali blocks, I told her she'll never get them but she went in and asked the man, and to my surprise he gave them to her. At the time my pickup had a small Hiab battery on it, and my wife was using it to load the blocks on the pickup. I remember I was sitting in the cab with my head held down while she was doing everything. I know it wasn't my finest hour and looking back I'm ashamed of my actions, but it all had to happen to make me the man I am today. Anyway because she was using the Hiab for so long the battery went flat and the pickup cut-out and because of the weight on the back of it, it sunk to the axles in the mockey grass and no matter how she tried the engine would not start. I remember I started effing and blinding and I said the hell with everything; I grabbed my three children and walked on and left her with the pickup. She was trying to tell me to try and give her a help, but I walked off in a huff. She had to walk on by herself to find a recovery yard. She found a man to give her a tow. She loaded all the blocks on by herself and got the man to tow her out; she drove down the road and collected me and the children. She's definitely some woman to put up with me but when I realised what I had done to her and when the shame finally hit me, this ended up being a turning point in my life because after this I became determined to pull myself together.

Anyway, when Bridget went to the recovery yard she had seen an old van lying up in the corner; she told me about it, but at the time it was like talking to an old boot because I had a zero attention span. However, after a few weeks when I had sorted myself out and got a little bit of a grip, I went back and bought that old van. I ended up selling my pickup, but I'll tell you one thing: that old van was the luckiest motor I've ever owned; I could literally drive to the garage and find a £100 chucked on the ground, it really was that lucky. Because of that old van I became a different man, I found the more I worked the better I felt. Depression is an awful thing – without warning it grabbed a hold of me. I've often heard people saying pull yourself together, but it's a lot harder to snap out of it than people think. I often likened depression to sitting in a car that has no steering wheel and no brakes, and the car's going about

20 miles an hour; then as you look out you can see people trying to tell you to stop, but what they can't see is that you are absolutely helpless and you're just not in control of the car, and that's just a little analogy of how I felt at that time, helpless. Anyway I struggled for years but I believe eventually I did learn to live with it, but from time to time when I think what I put my wife through and how she helped me, I do spoil her rotten because without her I would not be the man I am today. She got me on the straight and narrow, thank God. Anyway, when you go through depression it changes something inside of you, I suppose it's different for everyone but it made me into a workaholic. I was in a way, I did not like to sit down for a minute, it seemed the more I worked the better I felt, but sometimes no matter how hard you try, the universe just works against you. For instance, I remember getting this big job in which I had to move at least 10 tonne of mixed rubbish. At the time my father had a 10 stud cargo lorry with a double dropside tipper body, so to make life a bit easier I decided to lend it off him, but when I got to the job with the lorry, the height of the body made it very difficult to shovel and wheelbarrow the rubbish, so I made a makeshift ramp out of scaffolding boards. I put them coming off a wall onto the lorry, then I would fill the wheelbarrow and then take a run up the boards, tip it and repeat. On about the fifth go, the scaffolding board went from beneath my feet, and I fell a good eight foot to the ground, my leg bent back up and my knee dislocated. There was a sharp pain but as I moved the leg it folded back into place so I thought nothing of it and I finished the job. I was limping a little bit but by the time I got home my leg was black from my hip to my toes; the pain was excruciating, when I got on my seat I couldn't move, and to make matters worse that night my wife decided to go to bingo, she left me in agony with my leg, and on top of that I needed to go to the toilet – it ended up being the longest couple of hours of my life. I was turning purple, I couldn't move on account of my leg and I genuinely thought my kidneys were going to bust, the sweat was running out of me. I had to wait till my wife came back so

she could help me out to the toilet – the relief was something else lol. Anyway, the next morning my father and a couple of the boys lifted me out to the car and brought me to the hospital. I could not move my leg or my toes so the doctor thought I had done something to the bottom of my back. I said, "Doctor, I didn't hit my back though," and he said, "wait for a minute and I will try something". He got a syringe and started taking blood out of my knee cap, he took nine syringes full and then the feeling came back in my leg and I got the movement back. I was very relieved. The doctor said that I had torn all the ligaments in my knee. I didn't really understand what he was saying so I said "thanks, sir" and got out of there. I never went to no follow-up appointments, but thank god I never had a problem with the leg again. The very next morning I was on crutches but I still had to carry on working – it was the only way I could feel a little bit normal – and yes my wife never lived this down for the last 20-years: I always tell her how she left me suffering while she went to bingo, but all she does is laughs at me, but the truth is that a woman just can't understand a man's pain.

CHAPTER 5

ANYWAY MOVING FORWARD, IT was 2001, I remember I was at home watching a bit of telly, I heard a car pull up and when I looked out my window I could see Bridget's uncle Patrick, his face was white, I knew straight away there was something wrong. I said, "Patrick what is ever wrong?"

He said, "There has been a tragic accident and little Thomas was involved and he is very bad in hospital." He said to me, "You've got to get your wife and make your way to the hospital straight away."

At this point I knew it was serious so I left the children with my mother and jumped in my car and flew straight through to Wakefield hospital. When I got there things were looking bad, everyone was crying. I sat down with my father-in-law Wacker and I tried to comfort the man the best way that I could, but the poor man was hysterical. Anyway after a couple of hours the doctor came out and said that Thomas might need a blood transfusion – "is there anyone willing to give blood?" Everyone said yes straight away including myself, and God help us the doctors tried everything they could to save his life, but after a couple of hours the doctor came out and told my father-in-law that his son had died. He let a scream go that I will never forget, the pain in that man's voice was unbelievable; it was the saddest thing I ever heard. Thomas was only 25 years old, it was a crying sin for my poor wife and her family. I was saddened myself because Thomas was a very good friend of mine and at the time I felt a big loss.

Anyway, I moved back up to Yorkshire until after the funeral. It was a sad time so I gave my wife all the time she needed. When she was ready

I came home to Swansea. I tried to wrap my mind up into work and my wife tried to wrap her mind up into the children – you see, no matter how bad of a loss you have in your life, you've still got to move on; it's hard, but true. Anyway a couple of months later I was getting on with my life and one morning out of the blue a cousin of mine told me that Sonny was training for his rematch. I looked at him and said, "Do you know something, I am going to put an end to Sonny once and for all." When my cousin looked in my eyes I don't think he liked what he saw because a look of fear came onto his face, he was nearly crying. I said, "Calm down it's nothing to do with you."

"I know," he said, "I just don't want to see anyone get hurt."

I said, "Don't worry, everything will be alright."

Anyway the next morning I went through to Bristol where I heard that Sonny was supposed to be. I looked everywhere for him to finish the fight, but I could not find him. The next day when I got back to Swansea one of the men said to me, "Sonny knows you were looking for him." The man went on to say that Sonny had tried to get a gun for me. I looked straight into the man's eyes and I said, "If he wants it like that, it's not a problem, tit for tat."

My cousin Steven

Anyway, the next morning me and my father were sitting chatting, it was a beautiful summer's day and one of my cousins come to my father and told him that his nephew Steven had been killed in a car crash in Bristol – he was only 22 years old. My father was devastated, as was I, because Steven was not only a cousin, he was one of my best friends growing up; it was a big loss to the family. Anyway, two nights before the funeral I was in the pub chatting to a few of my cousins, and as I glanced over I spotted

Sonny walking in. Now my brother Michael and our Bucky were playing a game of pool; he didn't see me sitting in the corner so he tried to bully my little brother Michael – Michael was only 15 years old at the time. Anyway, when I stood up Sonny's face went as white as milk and we took to staring at one another across the room, not breaking eye contact for a second. After about a minute he looked to the ground; I knew he'd bottled it. I walked over and hit him a punch into the temple and I slapped him off the bar, he fell to the floor with blood running down his face. His family in the pub carried him out to his car and rushed him back to Bristol. Anyway at six the next morning I drove straight to Bristol to finish this once and for all – listen, I had something in my motor and I wasn't messing about; at this point it was beyond a fair fight in my eyes. Anyway after a lot of searching I finally found Sonny's house. I immediately blew the door off its hinges with a kick and ran in like a lunatic, but there was only a little boy on his own and as soon as I realised that there were no men in the house I turned on my heel and got out of there, but when this got back to Sonny what I had done, he panicked and tried to call a truce. He said, "Because of everything that was going on will you leave it go."

Listen, I will tell the truth in all honesty and full heartedly I did not want to let it go, but my father and grandfather came to me and explained that my poor aunt Mary was going through enough and she did not want no trouble at her son's funeral, so I reluctantly said fair enough. Listen, understandably there was a bit of tension at the funeral, but it went off with no trouble and Steven had a good send off after everything was done. I wouldn't hear from Sonny for some time which maybe was a good thing because considering the depression I was suffering and the frame of mind I was in at that point in my life, anything was possible.

CHAPTER 6

ANYWAY MOVING FORWARD, IN September 2001 my brother-in-law James Joyce Willy Boswell and my brother Bucky were going on holiday to France and out of good nature they asked me and my wife to go. The boys were just trying to cheer me and Bridget up a bit because at this point people knew I was depressed and also Bridget had just lost her brother Thomas, so I thought it was good of the boys and thoughtful, so for a laugh I said "no problem I'll go". I got Bridget to get everything ready that we needed and because my daughter Thoots was only a baby I left her with my mother and father and I brought my two sons to see Disneyland Paris. We got in Willy Boswell's Mercedes because that summer was boiling and he had some serious air conditioning – poor old James went in an old Sierra diesel and my brother Bucky had a small van . . . I'd say they were tortured on the journey over with no air conditioning. Anyway when we got to France we settled everything in the hotel and left the motors in the car park, we went on the French tubes and James Joyce was our navigator; in fairness we would have been lost without him. We went to Disneyland Paris with the children which was lovely; there was a ride there called Honey I shrunk the kids – it was very realistic: they shrunk the audience down into a matchbox, you could actually feel the dog's spit on your face and even the sensation of rats running over your feet, the children loved it. The next day we went to visit the Eiffel Tower, me and my brother Bucky had a bet to see who could go to the top of it. I backed out at the second floor because it had glass floors and the stairs had all holes in them and you could see the ground, but fair play to our Bucky, he went straight to the top whilst I was glad to get down and get off it. We had a good laugh at the tower but just across the road there were big fountains with water pumping out of them, it was scorching hot so me, Bucky and James Joyce jumped in the water. We were having a good laugh and I ended up getting Willy Boswell to come in, but when the French police realised what we were doing they tried to get us out of the pool. However, we refused to get out and they weren't coming in to drag us out, but what they did do was to get a big water cannon and started blasting us with it – the power of the water coming out of the cannon was driving us at least one hundred feet. We had the best laugh of all time because the more they were shooting us the better it was, but after about an hour we had no choice but to get out and go as the police were threatening to lock us up. It was a hell of a day though. When we got back to the hotel my brother Bucky realised he had not paid for a ticket on his van and his van had been towed away; it was very complicated to get the van back but thank god we sorted it and got it back. Anyway, that night in the hotel we were all drinking 99% proof shots – a half a glass was getting everyone drunk! We had a good time at the bar, but when I got back up to my room I heard people arguing. I looked out my window and you could see the roof of the hotel, it was all glass, then all of a sudden I saw a TV getting chucked straight through a window; it smashed a couple of panes in the glass roof, it must have caused thousands of pounds worth of damage. As usual we got the blame because of us being travellers, but thank god it was all on camera and we were cleared. As a matter of fact it was actually a Russian man arguing with his wife, and you know something: for once we got a full apology from the hotel which was nice.

Anyway, the next day we went sightseeing and we got on a big wheel, something similar to the London wheel; it had a full glass floor and no exaggeration it was a good 200 feet up. Willy Boswell and my brother Bucky were making a laugh, saying that I was a scared. Listen, fair enough, I don't like heights, especially like that, but they kept on and on, but little did they know at the time I was very bad with my nerves and deep down I didn't care if I lived or died. So I jumped up and started jumping on the pane of glass, trying my best to break it. I kept jumping and jumping; everyone's face went white and the boys started begging me to sit down. I said, "Now youse will stop." They went as quiet as a church mouse. When I got off I apologised to the boys for flipping out when they were only having a laugh, but what can I say – I was going through some very funny emotions at the time and my head was all over the place. Anyway, the next day we all made our way home but it was a cracking holiday – the only thing spoilt it was me being a fool for a few minutes in the glass wheel but I don't think the boys passed any heat to me because they were giving me some stick in all fairness lol.

Anyway, I was home about a week and me and the wife decided to go to the garage for a can of pop. When I got to the garage my brother Peter or Bucky and my brother-in-law James were in there chatting. I got my pop, saluted the boys and got back in my car. I had an estate Escort at the time, but as I drove out of the garage a man stuck his finger up to me and wouldn't let me out into the traffic. Listen, I blanked out, I don't even remember doing this, I'm only going off what the boys told me. Apparently I drove flat out and smashed into the back of the man's motor. I overtook him and stopped then I put my car in reverse and kept ramming him repeatedly. I left the man smashed up on the middle of the road. When I got back to the site I came around to myself and realise that I had smashed up my own motor, and when the boys got back all they could do was laugh; they said, "Jimmy, you are stone mad." I had to laugh myself at how stupid I was but it didn't feel funny at the time with my old motor smashed up for nothing.

Anyway, moving forward, what was to happen next got me thinking of the 90s where at that time me and my father had a lot of arguments and fights with different people, but due to respect those disagreements are not mentioned in this book. However, at the time there were people cut up, stuff rammed, stuff burned, some people were even shot; but we all gave as good as we got and there was no police involved and for that I salute them. When I settle an argument it is settled and that is the end of it. You see when I was young I was very thick and stubborn, I did not have a reverse gear. I'll give you an example of my mindset back in the day: listen, I was working once in Evesham and I dropped in to see my brother Peter. It was late afternoon and I was standing out chatting to the boys, when a travelling man drove in and he mistook me for someone else. He jumped out of his car with a double barrel shotgun, he pointed the gun at me and told me he was going to blow my brains out. I grabbed the barrel of the gun and stuck it to my forehead. I screamed at him to shoot me, I carried on that bad that the man got a fright and let go of the gun, I got it and hit him in the face with the butt and run him off the ground. Later on in life I often wondered what went through his mind after he left, he must have thought I was a madman, but that was just my mindset at the time, you see; to be old and wise you first have to be young and foolish. The truth is if I met most of them today we could go to a pub and get drunk together and there would never be an insulting word.

Anyway, the reason why I bring up some arguments that happened in the 90s is because one was about to be resolved. A couple of years beforehand my father had an argument with a Connors man that was left unsettled, but like my father always said, two mountains won't meet but two faces will. Anyway, one day my brother Peter was in Briton Ferry site and this Connors man drove in with his brother. My brother Peter said to him, "my father is going to give you a hiding when he gets you", and the man looked up and says, brazen like, "well now he knows where I am". Peter said, "Ok, I'll phone him to come over." He phones my father and tells him he has just seen the man that he is looking for, and my father shouted me through the site and says, "let's go, that Connors man is over in Briton Ferry". We speeded out and drove onto the site and right enough he was standing out. My father said to him,

"Are you the same man as you were before?" – "yes," he says, "I am". My father and the man pulled off their tops and got stuck into one another. It was a good fight for about seven or eight minutes punch for punch, but my father was too strong and he started dropping the man and driving him back with power punches, but what the man didn't realise is that even if a man gives best my father won't stop until he is satisfied that he's had enough. The man was trying to give best, but my father wasn't having it – he carried on beating him regardless; even when he fell to the ground my father kept on beating him, he beat him senseless. At this point his brother tried to intervene. I said, "what are you doing?" and he shouted, "your father is going to kill him". Well to be fair, he did have a point, because his brother was getting some beating, but the way I seen it, his brother should have thought about that before he put his self in a fighting man's place. Anyway, I pushed him back out of the way and then the fool put up his two hands and tried to fight me. I looked at him and laughed, but this little fella was supposed to be a good boxer – well so I heard but I didn't care about things like that. I said, "If you want it, you've got it." Without hesitation I hit him a left hook onto the right arm and snapped the bone in his arm, it flopped about like a wet noodle. I followed up with a right cross followed by a left hook and knocked him out cold; meanwhile, my father carried on beating this Connors man until an ambulance came. The ambulance crew put the man on a stretcher, and I kid you not, my father was still punching him while he was getting carried to the back of the ambulance! This man was brought to hospital where he was put in intensive care, fighting for his life. Two weeks later he came round – I heard this from someone that was in the room. The people at his bedside tried to say that we all jumped him, because of the hiding he got, but fair play to him, he looked up and said, "No one beat me, only Willy, the boys never put a hand on me." There was no police involved, they took their hiding like men; you'd have to give them respect for that. We never saw nor heard of these people again. Looking back on that fight with my father and that man, truthfully I have never seen a man get a worse hiding before that or since it.

Wacker and Anne harty

Anyway, moving forward, in October 2002 my fourth child was born; it was a boy, my son Jimmy. Not long after, in November, I got some news about my father-in-law. You see, after his son Thomas died, Waka moved back to Ireland. Anyway, one morning my brother-in-law Willy Boswell rang me at about 11am and he told me that "Waka took a heart attack through the night and was found dead". At that moment I was shocked but I then had to break the news to my wife Bridget that her father had just passed away. I broke it to her gently but she was devastated so I decided to leave the children with my mother and to bring Bridget to Ireland to fetch her father back, so he could be buried beside his son Thomas. On the way back we took the fast boat but it was the roughest boat ride I've ever seen – there were plates smashing, people literally getting slapped off the side of the boat, life jackets were handed out to everyone. There was a bit of a panic over the size of the waves but thankfully we got back and gave Waka a good send off. He was a gentleman, an old-time character that unfortunately are dying off in this day and age, they don't make them like that anymore. I just wish my children could have got to know him a bit better because he was a comical old man that I had good respect for. He died of a broken heart; he always lied about his age so when he died no one knows for sure what age he was.

CHAPTER 7

ANYWAY, MOVING FORWARD, IN the summer of 2003 I bought a new single wheel hobby off my brother-in-law Willy. He was in a camp in Leicester with my brother-in-law Ozzy, so I had to drive up from Wales to collect the trailer, but when I got to the camp the weather was beautiful. I remember it was absolutely boiling so I thought to myself the trailers in the camp and my poor Bridget had just lost her father, so I thought it would be a nice break for her to spend a couple of weeks with her family. It was good fun until one day Ozzy asked me did I want to come for a spin in his convertible BMW. I remember it was really hot and he had the roof back so I thought it would be a good idea to jump in to cool down, but I got a bit more than I bargained for because he took me down lanes at 140mph. I let on it didn't bother me, I said "put your foot down, Ozzy, go faster," and he laughed and joked about it but I didn't find it so funny, to be truthful; but when we got back to the camp he was telling Willy how fast his car was, he was trying to get me to back his words, but I started laughing and I told him straight. I said, "Ozzy, I will never get in a car with you again." He laughed, but the truth is he nearly gave me a heart attack. I can take a bit of sport but at that speed you're literally risking your life. Anyway, I had a nice couple of weeks' break and I enjoyed Ozzy and Willy Boswell's company, but I was glad to get back to Swansea.

Anyway, when I got home me and my brother Bucky started working together. I remember our Bucky got a job to move about four tonne of breeze blocks. At the time he had a short wheelbase transit van and when we got to the job Bucky reversed the van into the man's drive, I jumped out and opened the two back doors, and then we started loading the breeze blocks. No exaggeration, we stacked them to the roof. Me and Becky stood back in awe because we could not get over how good of a weight carrier the van was. I said, "Bucky, that van is unbelievable", but little did we know that when I opened the doors, I left one of them on the man's wall and as a result the van couldn't go down. Anyway, as soon as I noticed it and told Bucky he started laughing, and he said "that's why the van didn't show its weight", as he giggled; but in a moment of brilliance I said, "jump in the van, Bucky, and pull forward and it will come off the wall"; but when he pulled the van forward he put his foot down and the full wall fell down, the van fell on its axles and barely pulled out of the drive. It's funny looking back but at the time it was costly because we had to rebuild the full wall for free. We joked about it on the way home of how stupid we were to believe we could put four tonne in the back of a single wheel van – common sense there was something up, lol. Anyway, when we got back to the site this Riley man came over to me and my brother and told us he knew where a job was. I heard around that this fellow was a bit arrogant but I took no heed. I said to Bucky "we could do with a day's pay to make up for the wall", so I said to the Riley man "let's go, kid". We went to the house but the job was no good, the fellow had said more than his prayers, he had brought us on a fool's errand, so on the way back me and Bucky were cracking a joke like brothers do and this Riley's fellow picked me up on something stupid, so I said "you can't be serious", and he said "go and f... yourself". Well that was all I needed to hear, this was when we were driving back into the site, by my father's place. So I said, "Pull in there and get out, you've got to fight." I jumped out and sure enough he jumped out and put his two hands up. I hit him a sharp one-two and drove him on his ass with the blood skating out of his mouth. He got back up; I hit him a right hand and a left hook and knocked him unconscious. My father stopped me at this point and said give him a chance. At the time his mother was living on the site and when the woman heard the commotion she and the man's wife came running over to see what was going on, so my father calmed the women down, and then he got the man to his feet and the man walked over home with his wife. I walked over to apologise to his mother because I had good respect for the old woman, but as I was talking to the woman, he jumped into his pickup and started giving me cheek out the window, so I said "when I get you up the road I'm giving you a few bangs again". He skidded off up the road, at this time I started fuming; me and my wife jumped in my pickup and flew after him. I managed to pull him in but he would not get out of his motor. I remember I opened the driver's door and grabbed him by the jumper and I started punching his brains in. I nearly blanked out in temper. There was a lump hammer in his door panel, I grabbed it and drew back my arm, I was just going to let him have it in the head – and then my wife grabbed the handle and said "woah, you're going to kill him". The truth is he was very lucky: only for my wife was there I would not have stopped. He was left hanging over his steering wheel with the blood running out of him, I put him off the site that day and he moved to Newport. I saw him years later and he said he was sorry for what had happened, so I said fair enough and now today we are good friends. Me and Bucky carried on working together, every day we would go out, Bucky would collect weapons – there were more knives and daggers under my seats and behind them . . . if a policeman ever pulled me in at that time I would have got jail lol. We had some good laughs working together though, I remember this one time I was in a garage putting diesel in my pickup, this big bodybuilder kept giving me dirty looks, so I'm thinking what is this man's problem; but little did I know behind my back Bucky was making a laugh of the man, but when I looked at Bucky he seemed to be minding his own business and when I looked back at the man he was getting angrier. I looked up and shouted at the man. I said, "What is your problem?" Now behind me Bucky is laughing his brains out, he was putting his fingers up to the man. Now at the time I didn't see this, so as far as I'm concerned the man is trying to fight me for no reason. I looked at the man and told him "get going, I said or I'm going to knock you out", but the man wouldn't listen. At this point he is going ballistic, he runs at me with a wheel brace. I had a pick handle in the door of my pickup, I grabbed it and hit him straight on the head with it. The man was left unconscious with the

Me and my brother Bucky

blood running out of him. As I walked back to my pickup I looked at Bucky – he was rolling around the pickup laughing, but I was panicking thinking I was getting locked up. I jumped in my pickup and skidded out of the garage and then he told me what he had done; it wasn't funny at the time and especially not for the bodybuilder, but eventually when I calmed down I could see the humour in it.

Anyway, with my bad nerves and Bucky's sense of humour, it was time we went our separate ways; it had been a bit of fun working together though. Anyway, moving forward I would have good days and bad days – depression just doesn't go away, but as I went along I was getting a grip of things. Anyway it was 2004 and I was out painting the body of my pickup when I looked over and I saw my grandfather and father walking towards me. My father said to me that Sonny had got himself into trouble with the McGinleys. I said, "I don't mean to be ignorant but it's nothing to do with me, Sonny got himself into it, he can get out of it, it's no good running to us to fight his battles for him." My grandfather told me straight, he said, "Son, whatever arguments you and Sonny have, that's a family matter, we all have to stick together now and defend our name." I thought about it for a few minutes and I said, "Fair enough, I'll fight for my name but I won't fight for Sonny." My grandfather shook my hand and said, "That will do, son." The way I was told is that Barney McGinley wanted to fight Sonny and a fight was arranged with me and Trevor. Listen, Barney and Trevor are big names today but back then I'd never heard of either of them, though I'd heard of their father old Aney McGinley; but in truth I wasn't bothered – I never go off a man's name because I've seen men with big reputations get knocked out with two shots and I've also seen men with no name put up the hardest fight you've ever seen. What I'm trying to say is just because I never heard of them didn't mean that they weren't good men to fight and because of that I trained very hard, but halfway through camp the argument got stopped and the fights were called off – a shame because they would have been two great fights, well me and Trevor would have been great but Barney would have beaten Sonny easily lol. Anyway, as far as I was concerned that was that; eventually though, me and Trevor sorted our differences and today we are ok, no thanks to Sonny.

Anyway, moving forward, a couple of weeks later I went travelling to Plymouth with my brother-in-law Willy Boswell and a few of the lads. It was a good bit of sport because every morning before we went to work we had the black pan out, we'd have a bit of home cured bacon and beans with a bit of hot crusty bread, and every evening when we got back we would do a bit of fishing. I remember out of us all, my cousin the frog was the best fisher – he once caught six fish one after the other. It was all fun and games and we were having a good laugh, but after about a week of going to the one river someone must have reported us because as I was walking back to the van out of the blue a man from the Environment Agency tried to stop me; he said, "I'm confiscating your rod because you were fishing without a licence." I said, "Mate, I never heard of such a thing." He got a bit cheeky so I said get lost, and I ignored him and got in the van but the fool stepped in front of the motor and he wouldn't move, so I started laughing at him, because being a traveller I was well used to this type of situation, but a cousin of mine was driving the van and he was only a young boy and before I could stop him he panicked and rode the man straight over. I said, "You fool, what have you done?" He said, "I just tapped him, he'll be ok." I said, "You're going to get me jail, you clown, just drive me home", but when we got back to the camp rightly so it was surrounded by police, though the man that got run over mustn't have mention it to the police because he was carrying on like nothing had happened. I even saw him in the crowd and he just smiled and winked at me; it was a very funny situation. But whatever he said to the police they were very upset because they literally ripped us off the camp and escorted us all out of the county of Devon; they told us not to return and they even followed us as far as Bristol before they left us go. By the time I got rid of the police it was late at night so I decided to make my way back home to Swansea. I remember my wife was pregnant with my fourth son and plus I had had enough of the travelling; I was glad to get home but while I was getting chased with the police all night my brother Michael was at a wedding in Bridgend and he fell out with a gypsy man. The way it happened is the argument started in the pub and then it was brought out to the car park. Now I've been told by a lot of people that this gypsy man was the best man of his name and that the man could have a fight. Anyway, my brother Michael took him out, and then the two men pulled off their tops and got stuck into one another; it was a good fight for about three minutes, Michael dropped him with a left hook, the man was dazed but he managed to get back up, Michael hit him a sharp one-two and a left hook which sent him flying across the ground. Michael said "get up" but the man wanted none of it and he would not stand to finish the fight, so that night my brother claimed victory. But Michael wanted to give him a proper hiding so the next morning

Me my daddy and my brother Michael

at about ten, he came and knocked my window for me to see him fair play. I was tired after coming back late at night but I said "no problem, brother", and I jumped up. I remember me, Michael and a few of the lads went out to the people's site. When we drove in, there was about 40 or 50 men standing out, but fair play to our Michael, he didn't wait about – he jumped out of my car and said to the crowd "Where is the gypsy man that I give a hiding to last night because he's got to fight this morning?" The men looked up and said to Michael, "the gypsy man that you hit, he left early hours of the morning", so I looked up and I said, "is there any of youse that wants a few bangs because I'm here to fight as well?" but every one of them held their heads down and said nothing. Later on the same day they all left the site, so because of that we left it as a drunken argument and that was that.

Anyway, moving forward, not long after this my father was working on his lorry; he had this old cargo with a 650 square boom Hiab on it, he was working beside another lorry trying to lift the body off, but this old lorry had a faulty gearbox – when you turned the engine off sometimes it would drop into first gear by itself. At the time he had the two lorries pulled next to one another and, not thinking, he turned the old lorry off and when he did the gear lever dropped into first gear. Because he was busy he never noticed it and when he finished what he was doing he walked back to the old lorry and opened the door. He never thought to look, he just leaned in and turned the key, the lorry started and took off and it crushed him to the other lorry. He rolled the full length of the body, it crushed all his pelvis and busted his guts out through his belly. He fell to the ground, and out of shock he tried to stand up and walk but the bones of his legs come up through his pelvis and he collapsed. At this stage my mother was screaming and shouting, so me and all my family ran up through the site in a panic. I've got to be honest, I thought he was dead, I looked at his stomach busted open and his guts were hanging out, but thank God I'm a very calm person in this type of situation. I rang an ambulance straight away and tried to calm everyone down, but I was fearing the worst. The ambulance came and took him to hospital, I attended to my children and my wife, and then I followed up. He was in a bad state, he had multiple operations, pins and bolts, but thank god they stabilized him. I went up to see him the next day and when I got there he was lying on the bed, he looked in a bad way. There was a big lump under the blanket so out of curiosity I said, "Father, what's that?" He said, "Son, that's my privates." I said, "No way is that your privates." He said, "I'm telling you it is!" I said, "Give me a look then," and I was in shock – they were as black as a piece of coal and as big as two melons, he must have been in some pain. Anyway, later on the doctor told him that he would be in a wheelchair for at least two years. Now for anyone to get news like that it would be hard to take – but a man like my father that was so active and loved the gym: it was absolutely devastating for him.

Anyway I left my father and went back to the site and as soon as I hit the ground my wife was rushed into hospital to have my son Pio, but when we got in to the labour ward and the doctors looked Brigitte over I saw a look of concern on their faces and I got very worried – but when she asked me what was going on I told Bridget everything was fine and there was nothing to worry about; I didn't want her panicking. Anyway, early hours of that morning Pio was born; he was two months premature but even so he still looked a big fine baby so I was confused as to why the doctors were panicking so much. But what I didn't know was that when Pio was born he had a condition that caused his heart to pump the blood the wrong way around his body. I was confused myself when I first heard it, but the way the doctor explained it to me was that it meant that the child's lungs could not produce any oxygen, so because of that he was rushed into intensive care where he was put on life support. Anyway for five days my son Pio fought for his life but it was looking bad. I remember I was under serious pressure – I had my father in one hospital and my wife and son in another hospital. Later that night the doctor told me, "your son won't make it through the night", he said, "as the hours are passing he's getting weaker and weaker and there's no more we can do". My wife and I started crying, we were devastated. So I said to my wife, "we've got to get him christened". Now I don't know who got this priest but when he got to the hospital there was thunder and lightning, winds and gales; it was a terrible night. When this old priest walked in, god forgive me I had a very bad first impression of him – he must have been 90 years old, he had long yellow nails and to be honest he looked terrible, but the old man had come out of his way to christen my son so I gave him nothing but respect. Anyway the old priest walked into where the child was and he said to the nurse, "I've got to open the vent and touch the baby". The nurse took one look at him and said, "you can't touch the baby". He gave her a very stern look and said, "I've got to touch the child." He went against her and opened the vent on the incubator. Now all the machines were all level but when this old man touched the child the machines jumped up and down, it's hard to explain but hour-by-hour the child got better and better; the doctors couldn't even explain it. And what was weird to me was afterwards I tried to find that old priest to thank him, I remember I went and tried every local church and no matter who I asked no one had heard of that old priest; and to this day I never did know who he was, but I personally think he was an old angel. Either way it was a miracle sent from God.

Anyway, my son Pio was still months in hospital, but thank god from the moment that old man put his hand on him he never looked back and today he's a big, strong, healthy young lad and a good boxer as well. Anyway, moving forward my father was getting on well after his accident and he was starting to recover, but on top of all his troubles he got bad news about his father: the poor old man was given hours to live so I had to get my father and bring him to Bristol hospital. When we got there the hospital was packed with people. I walked past them, pushing my father in a wheelchair. I walked into the room where my grandfather was lying on his death bed, the poor old man was up talking but you could see he was just a bit out of it, obviously he was on a lot of medication. I remember it was very emotional for me and my father, so I shook my grandfather's hand and said goodbye to him – I did not want to wait in the room and see him die, so I walked out. I was sitting out in the waiting area and when I looked up I saw Sonny walking in. We locked eyes for a couple of seconds but he immediately looked away. I remember the look of fear on his face, but at a time like that I obviously wouldn't have said nothing, so I just blanked him. Anyway, a few hours later all I heard was crying – my grandfather had passed away; he was 77 years old, he was a great man and I had a lot of respect for him. Anyway, a few days later it was the night before the funeral and the family held a big wake.

Jimmy & Violet

Sonny and a few others were talking around a fire, but none of them noticed my 15-year old brother Martin. They carried on back biting my father for being in a wheelchair. Now apparently Sonny started saying that "there's only one man to beat now and that's Jimmy". He went on to say that my father was only a cripple – now bear in mind this is the night before his father's funeral. Listen, I understand Sonny is just that kind of a donkey, but the other family members that were having this discussion, well I think they should be ashamed of themselves, they must have had little on their minds; but fair play to my brother Martin, he started shouting, he said, "youse would not beat my brother Jimmy". I hear that Sonny actually went to fight my little brother, but credit to a cousin of mine, he said "if you hit that child you'll have to kill me". Out of shame one of my father's brothers stopped Sonny hitting my little brother – scandalous carry on! This argument was kept from me for a good five years, and to be truthful it's a good job because if I would have known at the time I would have gone up, especially in the frame of mind I was in, I would have cut every one of them in bits, I definitely would have got myself 20 years in jail – so it was probably a good thing that I didn't hear about it straight away. Anyway, the day of the funeral was emotional for me and my own family because it was hard seeing my father in a wheelchair as his father was laid to rest. Anyway everyone held respect and my grandfather had a very good send off. 2005 had been a hard year for everyone, but thank god my son was healthy and my father was still alive and at the end of the day you can't ask for much more than that.

CHAPTER 8

NYWAY MOVING ON, BACK in the 90s I met a man called Steve Lorey. We would become business associates but as time went on he has become something like a father figure to me. Anyway, Steve was having some trouble with a neighbour and he asked me to show him fair play so I said no problem. I drove up and collected him and we went to the man's place, I got out of my car and Steve jumped out and ripped off his top. I had seen this fella and I thought Steve was getting killed – he was a big man – but sure enough Steve hit him a straight right cross onto the bridge of the nose and dropped him, the man gave best straight away and Steve won his fight. I laughed at how fast Steve dropped him. I thought nothing of this but a few weeks later there was this big fellow on Steve's place. Now Steve is a man that doesn't care about anyone, but out of courtesy he gave me a ring to come up. I jumped into my car and went straight up. This man was standing there thinking he was something. I hit him a right-hand into the eardrum – Steve later told me that when I hit him it sounded like a shotgun blast, he was flattened with one punch, but when I looked at the man I noticed there was a bag of blood that came out of his eardrum. I'd never seen nothing like it before; it didn't burst but it was swelling. Steve looked at me and I looked at him – I think we both thought this man was going to die, so I escorted him off Steve's property. He staggered to his car and thank God I never saw him again. We always assumed that the man that Steve was arguing with paid this man to try and bully him, but needless to say Steve was never bothered again.

Anyway, this incident got me thinking and after some thought I decided to put my two sons into boxing, so I drove up to Mario Maccarinelli and asked him was it ok if my boys joined the gym. He was overjoyed and he said, "Jimmy, you didn't have to ask, they are more than welcome." My son Thomas was eight and my son Willy was nine – a good age to start boxing – but in truth it was not a way of life I wanted for my children; I didn't want my children to be fighters. A fighting man's lifestyle is a hard one, but when the shell of the egg is broken you can't fix it, when you start fighting you bring enemies, which become your children's enemies; it's a never-ending circle. So it left me no choice but to put my children into boxing. The first lesson I told my boys was never to show weakness, if you show weakness, I said, people will try and get up on your back. For instance I was at a Joyce wedding and I was standing out chatting to a few of the men, when this man walks over and starts giving it the big one to my brother-in-law James Joyce. James got aggressive at the man and the man backed down. I tried to be nice to him, I tried to calm the man down, and he started getting bold with me, because he'd seen my kindness as a weakness. He said when I start I'm like a lion. I smirked at him and thought to myself I'm knocking you straight out. I turned to James and I started laughing. I said, "Look at this fool," I said, "ok, lion man, throw your first punch." He threw a right-hand at me, I slipped the punch and hit him a sharp one-two and he dropped like a sack of spuds. I broke his nose and knocked his two front teeth out, the blood was pouring out of him; the lion was left crying, holding his two front teeth. Me and James walked away laughing. I walked into the reception and enjoyed the rest of my night. Later on, me and James and a few of the boys were laughing and joking about what had happened and James looked up and said, "well he definitely wasn't no lion". I laughed and agreed with him. Anyway the moral of the story is I put my sons in boxing so when they run into a donkey that thinks he's a lion they can defend themselves. But on a serious note, afterwards at this wedding a man was supposed to be bad mouthing me to one of my cousins, saying that Sonny would beat me. My cousin defended me by saying "my cousin Jimmy already beat Sonny". I think the man was just drunk at the time, but regardless, I still had to go out and pull him. I drove in to the Briton Ferry site and this man was standing out. I said, "Who do you think you are talking about?" He put up his two hands. I stepped to the side and hit him a right hook into the ribs; as he was falling down I hit him an awkward left hook on top of the forehead and knocked him spark out. He was brought to hospital in the back of an ambulance. I later heard that I broke three of his ribs and cracked his sternum with one punch. I've never heard of that man since, but what I didn't know at the time Sonny was going behind my back and claiming he beat me to everyone. Obviously people that knew me laughed at him, but if you tell a lie long enough and often, enough people will believe it. The truth is Sonny was just a stupid little man, he should have let sleeping dogs lie.

Anyway, moving forward, in the summer of 2006 my brother Bucky and Michael went out travelling. After a couple of days had gone by, my brother Bucky phoned me. He said, "Our Jimmy, I'm stuck, I need a tow." At the time I had a short wheelbase Shogun so I said, "No problem, brother, I'll be there in 20 minutes. When I got to the camp Bucky's trailer and his pickup were on top of a mound of grass and it was stuck to the axles. I reversed in and hooked his pickup onto the Jeep. My brother Michael told me not to attempt it because I would get stuck. I started laughing and I said, "How is this four-wheel drive going to get stuck? Don't worry, brother," I said, "I've got this." I skidded off and the wheels just kept spinning, the tyres filled with muck and sure enough my Jeep got stuck to the axles. At this point Bucky and Michael, they are rolling around the grass laughing, and I had to eat my words. I phoned my father to come and give me a tow; he had an L200 pickup with the big chunky tyres on it, but when he got there all he could do was laugh at the position me and Bucky were in. He put a chain to the front of my Jeep and towed us out like it was nothing. The boys made that much of

My brother Bucky with mommy and daddy

a laugh of me, I had no choice but to get rid of the Jeep – and I did love that Jeep lol.

Anyway, after a couple of weeks the boys moved back on to the site. The same night they asked me was I going to the pub. I said, "No problem, lads, give me a few minutes to get ready." I had a quick wash and a change of clothes and off we went to the Cross pub in Morriston. Me, Bucky and Michael were having a serious drinking session, so by about 11 we were well drunk. I looked up with double vision and saw five men walking in. I didn't notice at first because me and the boys were having a good laugh, but when the men got a bit rowdy I realised it was the same man that I had hit years beforehand with the snooker ball – he had come to try his luck. When he started giving a bit of cheek, I looked up, laughing. I said, "Did you not get enough the last time?" He replied, "I think you got me off guard." I started laughing. I was very drunk but I stood up and said, "Come here then and see what you can do." When he walked over he made a pitiful punch towards me. I hit him a right hand left hook and drove him straight under a table. I don't know if he walked in sober or he came back after some training, but he was beat easier this time than the first time and plus I was well drunk! I looked down at him under the table and I laughed because he was out cold and at this point Bucky and Michael had left the other four men in their own blood; I literally had to stop him from killing them. Me and the boys were stultified drunk and when you're in that bad of a state things can happen and I didn't want none of us with a murder charge, so I said, "come on, lads, let's get out of here". As I was walking out the door I looked around and everyone in the pub was knocked out. I pushed the boys out of the door and we done one, as we were walking on the path back to the site fallin' all over the place drunk, having a laugh. From the distance I could see a torch – the fellow with the snooker ball's face on him had got the police. I looked at Bucky and Michael, I said, "right, boys be calm and follow me". I went towards the police. The officer said "stop" and I let on to panic and said, "mate, they hit me a slap". He said, "Who hit you?" I let on to panic a bit more – "they're up there in the park, quick quick," I said. He let us go and ran up to the park, and we got out of there sharpest. My brother Bucky's wife picked us up by the roundabout at the top of the road from the site, the three of us were lying on our backs in the back of Bucky's van getting sick everywhere; we had a hell of a night. The next morning I went looking for snooker ball's face, and when I found him he started crying to me, he couldn't apologise enough. So I said, "Ok, don't ever give me or my family cheek again." The truth is that I was just glad to get home to nurse my hangover lol, but looking back it definitely was a wild night. At the end of the day it's good to make memories as long as it doesn't lead to jail lol.

Anyway, after this, to sweeten my wife up, I decided that me and her needed a break, so I booked a holiday to Spain, but on the way to the airport in Manchester there was a big storm with thunder and lightning which made me a bit nervous, but I sucked it up and got on the plane. However, the flight frightened me that much that I could not enjoy my holiday, I was stressed out the whole time I was there about the return flight. One funny thing happened though while I was there, me and the wife were on a boat and we sailed past this beach, this beautiful model of a woman walked out naked. I was laughing and joking to my wife, I said, "oh look at that" as I laughed, but as soon as I said it a man walked out from behind a couple of rocks – he also was naked so the laugh was back on myself: it was a nudist beach. I covered her eyes with my hand, she laughed at me and said, "it's not so funny when the shoe's on the other foot", as she giggled; she was having a great holiday enjoying herself. I tried to enjoy myself but my nerves were still at me – I couldn't stop thinking about the flight and to make it worse when I got back to the hotel room and put on the TV there had been a plane crash on the news, which made me even worse. My wife looked at me and she said, "Calm down, let's go out and relax beside the pool." I said ok but when I laid on the sun chair it was very warm and I fell asleep – when I woke up my legs were severely burnt. I was having one of them holidays where everything was going wrong, it was like one of them Chevy Chase films lol. When the day finally came to get back on the plane they brought us out on a bus and on approach to the plane I could see all welding and plates all over it, the plane looked antique, but I knew I had no choice so I reluctantly got on. When I sat down on the seat I caught my shin and because I had such a bad burn on my legs it ripped the skin off. I was in a hell of a state, on the way back I was breaking out in cold sweats; it was the worst few hours of my life. To make matters worse, there was still a big storm back in Manchester and there was localised flooding by the airport, and because the weather was so rough we had to land in Exeter. When we landed I literally kissed the ground and I've never been on an aeroplane since and it would take big money to get me on one again lol. Anyway, years later I would learn that depression gives you anxiety but I didn't know what it was at the time, I just put it down to fear of flying. Anyway, a couple of weeks later my brother-in-law Willy Boswell pulled down for Christmas and at least we had a lovely family Christmas which made up for the holiday that had made me even worse with my nerves lol.

CHAPTER 9

ANYWAY, MOVING FORWARD, IN 2007 I was working every day with Willy Boswell doing a bit of jet washing, one day after work me and my father and a couple of the boys were chatting out on a table and chairs, when a cousin of mine came to my father. We didn't know it at the time but this fellow was a proper trouble causer. Anyway, he told us that there was a family bullying him out the other side of Swansea and at the time we believed him, bigger fools us. Anyway we went out to these people at six in the morning, just to give them a warning, but when we got to the site there were no men there, and when we looked around there only was an old woman by herself. You see, unbeknownst to us the men had got up and left, so my father told the old woman in a nice way that he wanted to speak to her sons. Now, my father would never be disrespectful to an old woman, so he was gentle when he spoke to her, but I think her sons must have seen this as a sign of weakness and not as respect like they should have, but as we all know some people are really stupid and they have to learn things the hard way. Anyway, about a month later this cousin come back and told my father that the people were still bullying him and that they said that they didn't care about my father or his sons.

When I heard this it aggravated me. I thought to myself the cheeky bastards. Anyway, the next morning at six, we went back out to their site and as I drove in, there were about five or six men standing out. The leader of them was washing a car down – that was harmless enough – but when I realised that this time they stood their ground it angered me; though I was still willing to give them a chance so I jumped out of my car and walked over to the leader, but when I tried to warn him he looked at me as if I was a fool. That was his biggest mistake because I exploded in temper, I hit him a right hand and slapped him off the side of his car, it was a moment of madness. I dragged him to the door of his car, put his body in and I kept slamming the door on him. I'd only seen red and I did not stop until he was like a piece of bloody liver on the ground. Now at this point my brother Bucky got a plank of wood and beat this fella's brother to within an inch of his life. The rest of the men ran so we got back in our car and went down the road to another camp where some more of their family was staying. When we drove in a few of the men were standing out. As we jumped out of our car the one fella that was standing there, he was a bit of a boxer, I knew of him, he was well trained up. He put his two hands up to me, I hit him a front kick straight into the chest and slapped him off a car and as he bounced back towards me I threw a right hand and knocked him out cold; he was asleep beside the wheel of the car, his family was screaming and one of his brothers was coming out of a trailer. My father hit him a straight right hand as he was coming out the door and drove him into a toilet press, the women started roaring to get the police so my father said, "right, boys, get back into the car and let's go". As I was driving out a police car came facing me, I pulled down my window and told the police woman that was driving, I let on to panic, I said, "they're killing them in there, quick quick, hurry" and she said thank you and she let me go, and drove into the camp. I bet she felt stupid afterwards when they told her you just let them drive out lol. Anyway, I made my way straight home but the fellow that I hit with the door was brought to the hospital and he was put in intensive care fighting for his life. In truth I did go too far on the man, but because of all that I was going through I think I was gone a bit bad with my nerves, I was angry at everything, some days I just didn't want to see anyone and some days I was alright. The truth was I just couldn't control my temper.

Anyway, because of what I had done I had to go on the run for a couple of weeks, but eventually his oldest brother got in contact with me, he told me he was getting me jail. I told him straight: "If I'm going to go to jail, I'll do it for something worthwhile, I'll come in at three in the morning and burn youse to death in your trailers, I'll do my jail and I'll come out and do it again." This man was no fool and he knew that I was not bluffing. Anyway, about three days later all charges were dropped and as time went on we made up with those people and today we will say hi and bye if we see them. Sometime after this we realised that the cousin that had started this was a compulsive liar and a troublemaker; he was disowned from the family – he could have got us all life in jail over his trouble causing and story carrying. Anyway, after this, my wife and my mother sat me down and told me that they didn't want me arguing or fighting anymore, they said "you're going to go too far and get yourself big jail". I said to them, "It's not my fault that people keep picking on me and bringing me into their arguments." The two of them gave me a bad look so I said to them, "I'll get my mind in order and I'll try my best to keep out of trouble", but the truth is I was very lucky that I didn't kill that man and at the end of the day who would want to do something like that, so I knew I had to calm myself down and get my head straight – so I decided to go travelling with Willy Boswell. If anything I knew that he would

Me my brother Michael and our mother

keep me out of trouble lol. I was gone a couple of months when out of the blue I got a phone call from my mother; she told me that my brothers Michael and Bucky were in big trouble, she said that a week beforehand the boys were in a pub called the Star Inn, and this man insulted them, and when he did my brother Bucky stood up and knocked the man straight out. When my brother Michael had seen Bucky do that, he gave the other men a slap and put them out of the pub. Now the boys thought nothing of it, so not thinking a week later Bucky and Michael walked back into the same pub, but as they walked in they looked and there were seven or eight men just standing there looking, and then one man walked past the boys to the door and locked it. My brothers knew straight away that it was a set-up, because the man that Bucky knocked out the week beforehand had come out from the crowd and pointed to my brothers, and he said "they are the men that attacked me last week". Straightaway a big pub fight broke out Michael and Bucky were getting hit from all angles, Michael got into his stride and started dropping the men like flies with right hands and left hooks and anything else he could throw. Michael hit one of the men that hard that he snapped the man's jaw with just a single blow; there were kicks and punches coming in from every angle to my brothers, then all of a sudden my brother Bucky broke the leg of a table and he left two of the men in their own blood, he hit one of the men that hard that he cracked the man's skull. At the end up the boys were getting the upper hand so the men had no choice but to open the doors and run outside. Now the man that arranged this set-up, he phoned the police and got my brothers locked up. Anyway, a couple of days after my mother rang me, I came down to sort something out, but it was no good: the boys were still put back for a trial. Needless to say, it was a nerve-wracking few months but eventually the boys were found not guilty because at the end of the day there was seven or eight men against two, and because of that it was put down to self-defence. Sometime after the court case the pub was closed down and that landlord never opened a pub in Swansea again lol. During this case I heard the prosecution say how badly Michael broke the man's jaw, so as a joke I nicknamed Michael the jawbreaker and through the years it actually stuck on him – as a matter of fact more people call him the jawbreaker today than Michael lol.

Anyway, back to my story: while I was gone my brother-in-law Parr moved to Swansea and got a plot on the site, so for a bit of fun me and Willy decided to move back down to Wales. Anyway, one day after work me and Willy noticed that my brothers Bucky and Michael were rallying an old scrap Fiesta and it looked like good fun, so Willy couldn't help himself, he had to have a go. He asked my brother Bucky for a spin – Bucky said "no problem, carry on". Now there was this big bank down the bottom of the site, and

Me my uncle willy my nephew Billy and my son Thomas

in truth you would struggle to get a tractor up it, it was fairly steep, but Willy said, "I'll get the car up that". Me and the boys said "no way, you will kill yourself", but he said "stand back, boys and let me have a go". I smirked at him and said "I bet you won't do it". He jumped in the car and went up the road and he come back down at about 40 miles per hour. I stood in the middle of the road for a laugh and as he was coming towards me at the last second I jumped out of the way, he flew past me and hit the bank – he went straight to the top of it, spun around and came back down. The boys looked at me and said while they laughed "you was lucky, Jimmy, that he didn't hit you." I laughed and said, "I'm too fast, I'm like Bruce Lee." Everyone had a giggle and then Parr looked up and said, "I can do that as well." He jumped in the car and took a run at this bank. I was having a laugh so I did the same thing to Parr. I stood in the middle of the road in a karate stance, but Parr put his foot down and he was coming at me very fast. I left it to the last second and then I jumped out of the way, but I mistimed it, and as I jumped the car caught me on the leg and no exaggeration it spun me a good ten feet in the air. As I fell to the ground I was doing cartwheels, I was left broke up. Poor old Parr jumped out of the car as white as a corpse – I think he thought he had killed me but he had nothing to worry about because it was my own fault for being so stupid. At this time my brothers Michael, Bucky and Willy Boswell, the three of them were laughing their heads off. I didn't let on at the time but I was badly hurt. I was black and blue for weeks, but looking back I've got to admit it was pretty funny and if it would have been one of the other boys I would have laughed myself. Anyway Parr later told me he thought I was going to kill him but little did he realise when I got hit with the car I could barely walk lol.

Anyway, moving forward, in 2008 to keep myself out of trouble I wrapped myself up into work, but one afternoon my wife's brother fell out with a cousin of mine and he came and asked me to see him fair play, so I said no problem. On the morning of the fight my cousin had five or six men with him but that didn't worry me because none of them were my match and if I'm being honest I would have beat them all together, but as long as they knew their place I didn't mind them being there because as far as I was concerned I was only there to see fair play and that's what I was going to do. Anyway I choked the two men out and let them get on with it; neither of them were fighting men to say the least, but they had their fight and my brother-in-law ended up winning. However, unbeknownst to me one of the men standing there phoned Sonny to come in to watch the fight, but he was about ten minutes too late and as a result he had a dirty attitude. I think he was upset because he wanted my brother-in-law fouled and to be made to lose the fight, but when I see a man fair play regardless of who he is, if he's entitled to it he will get the win. At the end of the day fair is fair so I looked at Sonny and said, "What is your problem?" He smirked at me. Listen, I'm not a fool. I knew he had come in to make sure that his nephew won the fight, but I wasn't bothered about that, I had a score to settle with him, and as far as I was concerned there was no time like the present, so I ripped my top off and said, "let's have it right now". I said, "There's plenty of men here to see fair play, come on." His face went white and then he said me, "And you will never fight again, the last time we boxed every time you hit me my toes curled up." I looked at him and I said, "Well you want to lose that attitude then, Sonny, if you don't want to fight because I won't take none of your bullshit." He looked at me nervously and said "leave off the old trouble". I said, "You're the one, Sonny, coming in here looking for trouble with your chest out, but if that's how you want it fair enough." So I told him straight: "you stay your way and I'll stay mine". "Ok," he said and he jumped back in his car and left the site. I turned to a couple of the boys and I said, "That man is nothing but a donkey haha." Anyway I never saw Sonny for a while after that, you see what my wife and mother didn't realise is that being a travelling man is hard especially when you can fight, because you are expected to be a certain way so when they see you trying to avoid trouble they see it as a weakness; I suppose you could call it the law of the jungle if the lion shows weakness to the hyenas, he is liable to get eaten – some travellers are a lot like hyenas or donkeys as I would call them, show weakness and they are all over you. I was trying to keep my word to stay out of trouble but sometimes it's hard not to knock the donkeys out lol.

Anyway, moving forward a couple of weeks later I was out working and this lad called Patrick Price came up to me; he wanted me to see him fair play in Llanelli with his cousin JohnMichael Murphy. I said, "no problem". Now the two men had done a bit of boxing but they were not fighting men, but I will tell you one thing, for two average men it was one of the best fights I've ever seen, it was shot for shot for a good 15 or 20-minutes. The police came to stop it but I told the police: "It's a family dispute between two cousins, you're as well to let the fight finish." They said "fair enough" and let it go ahead. The police stood and watched it, it was a good scrap. At the end of the fight you couldn't pick a winner, they were very well matched, but JohnMichael managed to catch Patrick an uppercut and his head hit off a wall that he was leaning against; the force of the punch as well as his head hitting off the wall knocked him out. Patrick Price wasn't happy with the outcome so he asked me to arrange a rematch on my site in Swansea, and again it made for one hell of a fight – JohnMichael won his rematch but Patrick Price had nothing to be ashamed of, he had done a good account of himself. Some time after this Patrick Price lost his life; it was a shame, he was a nice young man.

CHAPTER 10

ANYWAY, ON A BIT happier note, later on in the year my wife hit me with the news that she was having a baby – it was the first time in a while that I felt happy, family life was good, my sons Willy and Thomas were doing very well in boxing, I was feeling very happy, and then out of the blue my brother-in-law drove in with a couple of the boys and told me that two

men wanted a fight at the top of the road. I said, "I'll come up and watch and if need be I will see you fair play", but when I got to the top of the road there were two big lumps of men standing out bouncing for a fight, there were about six or seven of us, but when I jumped out off the motor the boys stood back and the men ran towards me. There was nothing I could do, I had to get stuck into them, so I hit the biggest man a sharp one-two and dropped him, I spun on my heel and hit the other man a right hand and a left hook and dropped him. The other fella grabbed me from behind, I chucked back my head and posted his nose all over his face, he staggered back. At this time the other man runs into me like a bull, he grabbed me in a bear hug, I spun him to the ground and started punching him into the face, the other man picked a breeze block up and was just coming down onto the back of my head with it – he meant on killing me but thank god for Danny Connors, he ran over with a golf stick and hit the man on the side of the head, the man's ear was left hanging off; he actually saved me from getting my brains bashed in. I gave the men another few punches and ran them up the road with the blood running out of them, but credit to those two men, they never ran for the police, they took their hiding like men. Afterwards I told all the other boys that were standing watching, "I've a mind to punch the heads off every one of youse." Then my brother-in-law said nervously, "You had everything under control though, Jimmy." I said angrily, "This was youse a fight not mine, but youse won't come again." I said thanks very much to Danny Connors, he was the only man to come in, but when I got home this caused a bit of a domestic between me and my wife, and my mother wasn't happy with me either. The truth is I should have told them to fight their own battles, but at the time I wasn't thinking straight, so after this situation I decided to keep away from people that would get me into trouble. So I went to boxing shows with my two sons, they were fighting regularly and I had a nice quiet family Christmas.

2009 started off good, I was feeling much better in myself, I remember it was April my wife was out large having my baby girl Mouse. I had just finished work and my cousin Jimmy, aka the Frog, came visiting. We had a chat and a cup of coffee, then he said, "Do you want to go for a game of snooker?" He had beaten me in a game beforehand so I wanted revenge. I said, "Let's go, cousin." We went to the snooker hall in Morriston. I was beating him three frames to two, then I was just about to break the balls and this man called Davo walks over and pushed the snooker balls across the table. Now this fellow was a bit of a local bully, he used to bully all the other travelling boys and the local lads that came in to play snooker; he was a big lamp of a man but as the old saying goes he just tried to bully the wrong man. I walked over and hit him a open-handed slap, and I grabbed his two arms and twisted him up and pinned him to the floor. The other men in the snooker club started shouting, "get the police", I said, "you're beat," and I pushed him across the floor. I walked out slowly and got into the passenger side of my cousin's car, the Frog was driving. Anyway Davo walked out and the Frog wound down the window, he made a jab in through the car at me, I got infuriated and I jumped out of the car and ran at him, I threw a left hook as I was in the air and I connected him on the forehead, he hit off the side of a Vauxhall car and bent all the door in, the punch had left him with a three-inch gash on his forehead. The blood was pouring

down his face but when I hit him the bone of my arm went through my shoulder socket, my arm went numb and I could not move it, there was no pain at the time but when I looked over at him he was getting back up, my left arm was flopping about but I had no choice but to get stuck in, so as he runs into me I hit him a glancing right hand which put him off balance, I followed up with another right hand that connected him on his left cheek, I loaded up with a serious right hand and caught

Me holding my son pic after breaking my shoulder

him flush on the jaw which put him out cold. I looked down and he was asleep so I got back in my cousin's car and he dropped me straight back to the site. I said, "Thanks, Frog, see you later, cousin." I was glad to get into my shed to assess my arm. It was still numb and no matter how I tried I still couldn't move it, it left me very concerned. Anyway within 30 minutes my brother-in-law James drives into the site, he's got Davo on the phone, he said, "here, Jimmy, the man wants to talk to you". I answered it like a madman, I said, "The cheek of you to try and bully me." He was trying to apologise in every way he could, he said, "If I would have known it was you, Jimmy, I would never have done that." Davo knew of me but he'd never seen me before, well that was his mistake for trying to bully and that's why he got knocked out, but fair play to him, he stood up like a man and admitted that he was bang out of order; he said, "my face is broke up and you knocked me out, let's say I won't involve the police and leave it at that". I thought about it for a minute or two and then I said, "That's fair enough, but never give me cheek again." He said, "I definitely won't be that stupid." I wasn't in no humour for him to be honest so I said, "That will do, Davo, good luck," and I hung up the phone. I said, "Thanks, James, I'll see you after."

At this point I was more concerned about my arm than anything else, but I must have been in shock though because I never felt pain for a couple of hours, just numbness, I still couldn't move my arm, but just as I was trying to decide whether I should go to the doctor's my wife walks out and says, "Jimmy, I think I need to go to the hospital." I immediately forgot about myself and I got her into the car and made my way down to Singleton hospital. As soon as I got into the ward the pain started to kick in to my arm. My wife was going in to have the baby and I was trying to comfort her, but I've never felt pain like this in my life. After about four hours of excruciating pain I couldn't bear it no more – every time the midwife walked out I started taking the gas and air, Bridget was laughing calling me a druggie but I was in that much pain I didn't care, I just kept on sucking on the mask. I must have taken the whole bottle because it stopped working, the pain kicked back in, it was that bad it's hard to explain but I had no choice, I said, "Bridget, I love you, but you're going to have to stay in here by yourself because I've got to go back to Morriston hospital to get this sorted out." She seemed fine at the time so I left her and I made my way to the hospital. I was sitting in the waiting area and my friend Boris was in there, I was trying to talk to the man but then I started breaking out in cold sweats at this point, I was taking dizzy turns with the pain, and when the nurse called me in to be seen, as I stood up I fainted and collapsed; they rushed me in and thought it was only a dislocated shoulder and they tried to pop it back in, but they were unsuccessful. Once I got the pain medication I started to settle down and got a bit of focus back, I started to feel a bit guilty for leaving my wife on her own to have the baby, so I thought I'll have to get back to the hospital, so I sneaked out from the doctors and went back to Singleton hospital but when I got there she was getting ready to come home; it was the early hours of the morning so I thought she was just coming out because of me, so I said no you can't come out she said I'm ok, but I still had to go and ask a midwife what was going on because I didn't want her to hurt herself or the baby because of me, and thank god when the woman explained it to me it was only threatening labour, so I said to the midwife "thank you very much" and I went straight back to Morriston hospital, by the time I got there I was in serious pain but fair play to the doctors, as soon as I walked through the door they sent me straight down for an operation, but again it was unsuccessful. The doctor came into the ward and told me, "you've got to have open surgery to correct this problem", I said, "carry on, doctor, do what you've got to do", and it ended up being a seven-hour operation but thank God everything went perfect. The doctor said afterwards that I wouldn't get the use of my arm back for at least 18 months. I said, "Fair enough, doctor, but I do a lot of boxing, do you think I'll be able to box again?" He said, "If you do everything we tell you in physio, it will be a 100% and as a matter of fact it will be stronger than it was before." I felt a bit better hearing that, but at that time I didn't believe him.

Anyway, I was a few days in the hospital and not to show weakness to my enemies I decided to sign myself out. On the morning I was going home the doctors strapped my arm up on a cushion and placed it on my chest, and off I went, but when I got home I was sorry for leaving the hospital because the pain was unbearable, I couldn't sleep properly, I couldn't lie down the pain was so bad. I had to try and sleep sitting up, what little sleep I got. Anyway in the month of May my wife went in to have my daughter Mouse, but because of my arm I think I was in more pain than she was, because without a doubt it was the hardest delivery out of all my six children lol. Anyway, thank God my daughter Mouse was born perfectly healthy and after a couple of days mother and child came home, and as for me I was trying to come to terms with a terrible shoulder injury. I remember I never felt as vulnerable, even though I suffered with depression, I was always so fit and strong and ready for a fight, but at that time I felt so weak, then you had the opportunists or the donkeys as I would call them coming to try their luck – for instance my nephew Billy Harty, Parr's son, was pulled on the site with me, at the time he was only a young bit of a boy when one of my cousins, a full grown man, came in trying to bully him. My cousin was obviously thinking I could do nothing about it, but it turned out I didn't have to because my nephew Billy was no fool, he took my cousin out and beat him like an ass. I managed to come down and watch it, I was standing back laughing because I knew their game. When the fight was over I put my cousin off the site and as he was going I said, "I'm telling you, don't come back around me again". He went off with his mouth all busted and the blood running out of his nose. Anyway the next morning his father came down to the site, he was trying to throw his weight around, but even though I was feeling week I wasn't having none of it, so I walked over to him and I just told him straight, I said: "Do you think my arm is going to be like this forever?" I said, "Know your place or I'll put you in it." The look that came on his face was priceless, it was as if he had just realised who he was about to give cheek to, he went quiet and held his head down. I said, "I'll kill everyone of youse if you keep it up, now stay off my road and don't come around me no more." He knew I was serious, he never opened his mouth, he just drove off the site and he's never set foot on the site since. The truth is that the frame of mind I was in at the time, I could have easily murdered someone, because of my situation I felt like everyone was trying to take a liberty off me.

Anyway, a couple of months went by, I was still in a lot of pain, but thank God I had started to stand up and sit down a bit easier. I still couldn't move my arm but at least it was something positive. Anyway, I was in the town shopping and I got a phone call from Sonny; he was shouting down the phone telling me to get back straight away to the site. I said, "You wait there, Sonny I'll be back in 20-minutes." I drove in like a lunatic, I thought the cheek of him to try and start on me now, when he knew I was in such a weak condition. I crawled out of the car in pain, I looked at Sonny and he was laughing, I was in a serious temper. I said, "When I asked you to fight the other day, Sonny, why didn't you get out and fight?" He was letting on to joke when he knew I was extremely angry. He said, "I'm only having a laugh, I was just winding you up." The truth is he tried his luck and when he saw the look in my eyes he shit himself, and tried to get himself out of it by putting it off as if it was a joke, but little did he know I was prepared to do life in jail if I had to because I had something under the seat of my car and I would have killed him dead where he stood without hesitation, because even at my weakest hour I still wouldn't let Sonny beat me, or best me. You see, I would rather die on my feet than live on my knees, but at the end of the day, the truth is that Sonny's always been an asshole and because of that it was nothing new that he stepped out of line, when he thought he had an advantage, but what surprised me at the time was all the donkeys, at how sly and two-faced they can be, because when I was strong and fit, they were kissing my ass, and at the first chance they got when they thought I was weak they tried to take a liberty off me, but believe me I got every last one of them when my arm was better and I gave them all a bad beating, which in my opinion they deserved; but after I did, one of the boys as a joke said, "Jimmy you never leave nothing go" – but that's not the way I see it, I just don't forget about a bad turn or a good turn. I'll give you a couple of examples just to show how my mind works. When I first got married I was only a little boy of 17, I've already told you of the van that I put the diesel engine in that kept breaking down, well when I was putting the engine in, the snow was thick on the ground and this man by the name of Mickey Connors, saw me struggling by myself, he went out of his way to give me a help to put in that engine – that was a good turn in my eyes and I never forgot it. Twenty years or so later I was in a camp out travelling and Mickey's son had broken down with an old Escort Van, so I went out of my way to help that boy. I even had a mechanic to fix his van for him because I never forgot what his father had done for me, and when it comes to a bad turn I'm even worse. I was 19 years old and I was cutting up an old lorry chassis and I went to a mate of mine to lend an oxy bottle off him, and he refused me. I knew he had one so I looked at him calmly and just said, "you will come again". Sixteen years I had to wait and one day he came to me for a lend of an oxy bottle, and my words to him were: "Do you remember when you refused me when I came to you in an hour of need?" He let on he couldn't remember. "Well," I said, "that don't make any difference because I remember. You'll be getting nothing off me." The moral of the story is, if anyone does a wrong turn to me, if it takes me 20 years, I will get them back and I never forget anyone who does me a good turn. Come to think about it, maybe I don't let nothing go, but I believe on this occasion because of the circumstances I was 100 percent in the right to break them donkeys up lol.

Anyway, back to my story, it was a dirty move that Sonny tried to pull when he called me back to the site, and it was only a matter of time before it got back to the ear of my brother Michael, and when it did he went straight to Sonny and pulled him. Michael told him straight, "When Jimmy's arm is healed you can have your fight with him, but meanwhile I'll do Jimmy's fighting for him." Sonny was trying to crack a joke – "I was only having the sport with Jimmy" he said, but Michael knew what kind of a man Sonny was, so Michael just told him "don't have me to come to you again". Sonny held his head down and said nothing. After this Sonny went quiet for a time, so I tried to get on with my own life.

CHAPTER 11

IN FEBRUARY 2010 MY son Willy was fighting in Scotland in the British championships, so I let him go ahead of me with the British squad on an aeroplane and me and my son Thomas took the train – there was no way I was getting on a plane. When we got to Scotland everything went according to plan my son Willy won his two fights and became British champion. I was very proud so I got my two sons and got back on the train to come home, but on the way back down I got a phone call that my wife's mother had just had a stroke; my exact thought at the time was when it rains it pours. Anyway, I met my wife in Northampton and when we got to the hospital, the doctors said she had taken a massive stroke and she had no chance of coming out of it. My wife was devastated. Within a couple of days she lost her mother who was only 61 years old, it was a sin, she was a nice old woman, and a very good granny to my children. This was a hard time in me and my wife's life. I stayed in England until the funeral was over and then I made my way back to Swansea. Later on in the summer my brother-in-law Willy Boswell pulled back down to me to do a bit of work together. I couldn't do much over my arm so it was good of him. One day we were doing a job and I got a phone call from my brother Michael, he said, "Jimmy, you want to make your way out to Mummy's." I said, "What's wrong, brother?" – "Nothing," he said, "just come out to Mummy's, we're all here." I said "no problem" and I hung the phone up. I looked back to Willy, I said, "You carry on with the job, I'll have to go out just in case there's something wrong." Willy said, "no problem", so I made my way out but when I walked in to my mother's you could see where she was just crying and when I looked at my sisters they were also crying, so I said "what is ever wrong?". She said, "Son, I've been diagnosed with cancer and I'm just waiting on the results to see if it's the aggressive one or the calm one; either way, I've got to go for a major operation." As she was telling me this I was thinking to myself could things get any worse, but thank god a few weeks later she got the results and it was not the aggressive type. She went down for a big operation and thank god they removed it all, she was months on radiotherapy, it was a really hard time for the family, but especially for my mother because she is a proud woman, but thank god she would go on to make a full recovery and get the all-clear. I was certainly glad to see the back of 2010.

Anyway, moving forward, 2011 started off a bit better. I had the movement coming back in my arm, which at the time was very good but it still wasn't a 100-percent; as a matter of fact it felt like dead arm, you know when you sleep on it or lie on your arm for too long, it was exactly like that. Anyway, when I tried to move it I had no control and I still couldn't lift it above my head, but it was still a lot of progress because a couple of months beforehand, I couldn't move it at all, but as good as it was coming on I still didn't want to rush it so I just went with what the doctors were telling me.

CHAPTER 12

ANYWAY, IT WAS MARCH 2011, me and Willy were doing well out of a bit of work so we decided to treat ourselves to two new cars. I got a black VW Touran and Willy got a silver one. Things were starting to look up, and in June we decided to go to the Swansea airshow. Between me and Willy we had too many children to fit into the motors, so for something different and a bit of fun we took the bus. On the way down we had a good laugh, Willy started singing the wheels on the bus go round and round, everyone including the country people were in stitches. When we got down to the airshow the power of the jets and the display they put on was awesome, we all really enjoyed it. The next day Willy had to go back to England; meanwhile, a couple of the boys were in a pub and Sonny walked in and started bullying, he punched one of them in the face and then he slagged all night. The next morning this got back to my brother Michael and my father, so they went up to Sonny's house, Michael knocked on the door. He wanted to take Sonny out just for a fair fight and my father could see fair play, but Sonny wouldn't open the door, he was giving cheek and calling names out the window. At this point Michael got angry and was trying to rip the door off the house to kill Sonny. Sonny phoned the police and Michael and my father were escorted out of the housing estate, and were told by the police not to come back again. Later on, Michael was trying to arrange a fair fight but before he could get it on, there was a tragedy in the family – my brother Willy's little daughter Sarah Margaret passed away. It was devastating news. Anyway, the funeral was to be held in Morriston cemetery. At the time my father sent word to Sonny not to attend, but on the day Sonny still showed up. There were easily 150 people standing there. Sonny jumped out of his van with a black pair of gloves on, and my brother Michael said, "Right, Sonny, you were told not to come here, but saying is that you are here let's get this fight on." Michael ripped his top off and went to fight him, Sonny ran back to his van; he looked like he was trying to find something. At this point one of my family members had a gun in his coat and because of Sonny wearing gloves he thought that he was trying to shoot Michael; so, not thinking, my family member ran over, he never hesitated, he pulled the gun and fired it directly at Sonny, it went bang but it must have misfired because the bullet veered off into the side of the van, but with the noise of the gunshot the funeral broke out in chaos, people were running for their cars, women were roaring and screaming. In all the commotion Sonny must've got a very bad fright because he jumped into his van and left the graveyard, my family member got rid of the gun by chucking it in a bin, and within minutes the graveyard was surrounded by armed police. The truth is Sonny was lucky to get his life out of the graveyard, but in fairness if he had any respect he should not have been there in the first place. Anyway, at the end up, Sonny was left with no choice, he had to have a fair fight with Michael. The fight was arranged to take place in Pontardawe, Sonny had been training for months for this fight but my brother Michael is one serious man. Anyway, on the day of the fight Michael jumped out and ripped his top off, Sonny pulled his top off and then he said to Michael: "I'm knocking you straight out, you're no good to me." My brother Michael started laughing, Michael said, "Let's go then, Sonny, let's see what you've got." Sonny threw a right hand over the top, Michael stepped to the side and threw a right hand left hook, which connected Sonny on his left eye and just above his right ear. Sonny fell to his knees, Michael steps back and lets him get up, then he runs back in and hits him a sharp one-two and a right uppercut. Sonny was left hanging over the railings with the blood running out of

him. My father stopped the fight, he said, "Michael, he's had enough."
Sonny later said that Michael beat him in the best of fair play, but within
days Sonny had done a complete U-turn, he started saying that Michael
didn't beat him, but the truth is he's just a really sore loser. Anyway, later
my father phoned Sonny and told him straight, he said, "keep away
from my children now and stop looking for trouble". Sonny agreed on
the phone but what we didn't know at the time, after the argument at
the funeral, the same night Sonny went up and got on his knees at his
father's grave and took a promise that he would beat me or Michael
before he dies. Well up to this point he hasn't been doing too good on
his promise, lol.

Anyway, moving on, it was the end of July 2011 and my brother-
in-law Willy Boswell got really bad news – he was told that his nephew
and another lad had been killed in a car crash. It was a sin because
Willy's nephew was only 21 years old. Anyway this was sad old news so
I decided to go up to Willy and his family to pay my respects. When I
got there the field was packed with people, but what stood out to me was
that they had all the motors sign written with big photos of the two boys
that had been killed, which was a nice sign of respect but it must have
been hard for the family to look at. Anyway I tried to comfort Willy's
brother who had just lost his son, but when I looked at the man he was
heartbroken. I told him that I was sorry for his troubles but everyone
around me was crying. I felt awkward so me and Willy walked away
from his brother. I said, "I'm sorry, Willy, I didn't know what to say."
He said to me, "At a time like this it's just nice to see a different face,
my brother appreciates you coming here, Jimmy, and showing respect
and so do I."

We carried on walking and chatting, I remember there were a few
young boys speeding up and down the camp so we started fixing the
fences to keep all the small children in, and when we finished I went
over to my wife and I said, "Bridget, there's nothing really we can do
here, will we do one?"

"Ok," she said, "let's go." And on that note I said to Willy, "I'll see you at the funeral." He said, "Ok, but will you bring my son Lewis and my daughter Nicole back with you?" I said "no problem", we said our goodbyes and I made my way back to Swansea. The second boy was getting buried in Ireland so out of respect Willy went back to the funeral, the plan was later to come back to his nephew's funeral in Leeds. Anyway when Willy got back to Ireland that night he phoned me, he said, "Jimmy, I can't get a hotel room, they won't take cash, have you got a card?" I said no because I couldn't find my card, but he ended up getting a room in the same hotel as my wife's brother; anyway after a bit of sport with the boys Willy went out and got some Chinese food, then he said: "boys, I've got a splitting headache I'm going to go and lie down". He went to his room and after eating his food he had a shower and then he got into the bed and then he turns out to go to sleep, his wife turns out her way but when she did she hears Willy falling out of the bed. She said, "Get up, are you alright?" He never answered and she jumped up to see was he ok, but when she looked at him she could see blood coming out of his mouth. With the sight of that she panicked and started screaming and shouting. The full hotel came running to see what was going on, an ambulance was phoned and when the paramedics arrived they worked on him frantically doing CPR but it was no good: when Willy fell out of the bed he was dead before he hit the floor – he died of a brain haemorrhage, he was only 37 years old. When I got the news the next morning I was absolutely devastated, it was like losing one of my own family. I dropped everything and went straight back to Ireland. When I walked in and saw Willy in the funeral home I was overwhelmed with grief, I couldn't believe what I was looking at. It was a very sad time for everyone, his old family was devastated, his poor wife she didn't know what to do with herself. We brought Willy back to Leeds in Yorkshire, his family burial ground, and he had a proper gypsy man's send-off. Willy's brother's was trying to have me carry his coffin but I couldn't lift my arm up high enough so I had to walk alongside it, just holding the handle with my right arm. It was a sad day, Willy was one of my best friends and he is very sadly missed. On the way back from the funeral I busted out crying but I had to suck it up – I had a little family to look after and things to sort out.

Anyway, when I got back to Swansea I kept his son Lewis with me and put him into boxing with my boys. A few months went by and out of the blue my brother Michael and brother Bucky phoned me up and said, "One hundred per cent, lads, I'm ready to go." Bucky was in a great humour because he was working that day and he lifted a big axle onto the back of his pickup and this gypsy man after seeing it said something funny to him, he said, "Dodi Dodi chavvy." Bucky found it very comical. In the pub that night I had a good few pints of beer, I thought to myself at the time life was too short so why not, me and the boys laughed from going into the pub until the last bell. Bucky kept repeating what the Gypsy man had said to him, he made us laugh all night, at the time it was exactly what I needed to leave off some steam. Anyway, the next morning my brother Peter and a few of the other boys came over to ask me was I going for a picnic in the park. I had a serious hangover but I said, "Ok, let's go, brother." When we got there everyone was having a good laugh and a joke, but I looked over at this young boy playing on a skateboard ramp, I said to my brother Peter, "I'll bet I can do that", and he replied, "go away, you fool, you'll kill yourself". I said, "watch this", and I walked over and asked the young boy for a go of his skateboard. "No problem," the boy said. The ramp was all made of steel, I remember it was about ten foot tall and a good 30 foot long but it genuinely looked easy to me. I climbed up and stood on the skateboard. Peter and the boys were begging me not to do it, but I started laughing and said "watch this". As I went down the ramp the skateboard went one way and I fell about seven feet straight onto the broad of my back, I hit it that hard that I shocked the full steel frame, it took the wind out of me. I could barely breathe but when I did manage to look over at the boys and my brother Peter, they were rolling around the ground laughing at me. I didn't find it funny straight away but after a while I had to laugh at how stupid I was and especially having such a bad hangover. Well one thing for sure it definitely didn't help lol. Anyway, I was bruised and battered for days but whenever it's brought up it always brings a smile to my brother Peter's face, so because of that it was worth it, haha.

Anyway, moving forward, not long after this my son Thomas was boxing for the British title in Manchester, so I sent him up with the British squad and me and my son Willy drove up in my car. When we got there Thomas had already won his first fight and he was fighting for the gold. I looked over at this tall skinny black boy, I remember thinking at the time that my son Thomas was going to knock this boy out, but he was actually a bit better than he looked. It went on to be a good fight shot for shot for three rounds, Thomas lost by one point; he came away with silver but it wasn't bad considering he boxed Daniel Dubois, as of 2019 the current British champion and in my opinion the future world champion. My sons Willy and Thomas had done very well that year in boxing but the traveller way is hard to get out of and in early 2013 my son Willy went up visiting his girlfriend in Doncaster, he was off with the boys and girls in a nightclub and this little fellow Ambrose Dear hit my son Willy a sly punch through the crowd. Anyway, there was a big scene and everyone split them up, but the next morning Willy demanded that he had a fair fight. A nephew of mine told me what was going on so I rang my long time friend Valence Dear, who was the boy's uncle and as I was in Swansea I had full confidence that he would see my son fair play. It turns out that the apple didn't fall far from the tree, my son has the same gift as my father bestowed to his son's power, he made short work of Ambrose, Willy beat him within 20 seconds, by knockout. That afternoon I gave my friend Valence a call and told him thanks for seeing my son the best of fair play. When my son Willy came home I tried to advise him not to go into that way of life because it is too hard, I said, "Son, be a businessman, not a fighting man, it's not a good life, but if you have to fight be a world champion, you have the talent." He agreed with me but I was still proud of him.

Anyway, moving forward in June of 2013 my granny was rushed into hospital and given hours to live. The hospital was packed – I had not long done a documentary and me and a load of the boys were standing out having a chat about it, then Sonny pulled up in his car. The man had a dirty attitude, he got out steering like he wanted to fight. I blanked him at first out of respect for my father, but because his old mother was dying you would imagine Sonny would have had more on his mind, but he walked over and tried to snigger over the documentary, so I said, "why don't you go in to see your mother, Sonny, and stop with your attitude because your fighting days are long behind you?" and he held his head down and walked away. This was coming into a time of my life when I had more on my mind, my little family was growing up, so I had no time whatsoever for donkeys like Sonny. Anyway that afternoon my granny died, she was 83 years old. She had a good send-off. I don't recall seeing Sonny at the funeral but I was later told he was there.

CHAPTER 13

ANYWAY, AFTER THIS I decided to bring my little family away for a break, so in September I brought my wife and children to London where we booked into a mobile home for a week. We really had a good time, we went to Madame Tussauds, Chessington World of Adventure and LEGOLAND, we had a good family holiday and then we had a quiet Christmas. In February of 2014 me and my wife were having a quiet few drinks and a bit of food in the Dylan Thomas bar and restaurant, at about 9 p.m. I looked up and there was Sonny walking in with his wife. I looked back and said to my wife, "Look at this, guaranteed I have to knock him out tonight", but surprisingly he was civil and was talking sensible at first, but after about an hour he made a slight remark about my arm. I laughed at him, I threw a few combinations just to show him that my arm was fully healed up, but before anything could kick off I asked him straight, I said, "Sonny, why do you keep looking for trouble with me, why can't you just bury the hatchet and move on with your life?" Now if you said this to a normal man they would probably shake your hand and agree with you, but he actually took this as a sign of weakness. He got a little bit aggressive, he smirked at me and said, "I'll see you later", and got up and left the pub. I looked back to my wife and told her "I can't work that man out". I thought nothing of it at the time but a couple of months later I was standing out chatting to my cousin Mano and then Sonny drives in, he was well drunk, he had a terrible attitude so I said, "why don't you go home and when you sober up you can come back".

He said, "Who are you giving orders to?"

I replied, "Less of your cheek, Sonny, you're drunk."

He looked at me and said, "I'm the best fighting man in the country."

I said, "You can't be that good because I've already beat you more times than once."

"Yeah," he said, "but I never give you best."

I held my hand on my forehead and took a deep breath and said, "If you keep pushing you're going to get yourself into another fight." I gave him every chance and he still didn't take it. At this point my wife walked out of my trailer, and he called her out of her name. Well that was it, I went mental, the boys had to stop me from hitting him. I said, "Sonny, I'll be at your house at six in the morning."

"That will do," he said and he drove out.

The next morning me and my wife drove up to Sonny's house. I was there for 5:50. I knocked his door and he opened it. I said, "Are you the same man as you were yesterday?"

"I am," he said.

I said, "Get out here into the garden."

He walked out and put up his two hands, I hit him a sharp one-two, he staggered, I hit him a double right hand and a left hook, he was out on his feet leaning against the wall; as he stood up I threw a vicious right uppercut and put him out cold, in his front garden. I told his wife, I said, "When he wakes up you tell him do not come around me no more." Me and my wife jumped back in my car and drove home. I was standing out with my brother-in-law James telling him what had just happened when Sonny drives in, in his van. He jumps out with a bread knife at least a foot long, I think he must have drank a full bottle of whiskey on the way down to the site, or the punches I hit him with must have put him scrambled; either way he was all over the place, he tried to come at me with the knife but I closed my gate and went back into my plot. He started banging the knife off my gates and walked off the site. Now in my opinion he must have fallen on some plant equipment up the road, because he gave himself 214 stitches in his left arm and he had to have a plastic elbow fitted. Either way he was rushed into Morriston hospital where he lost a lot of blood and was in shock; he was defibrillated four times because his heart had stopped, he was put into intensive care and at one point he was on life support because his lungs stopped working. The police would later say that I was supposed to have cut him up with a samurai sword and beaten him half to death with a shovel, but that was all lies, I don't know what happened to him, I know I beat him and knocked him out at his house in his front garden, that is all I know and that is what I told the police. Anyway, the incident occurred on the 19th of April, and on the 20th Sonny's wife gave a statement to the police. She said, "Jimmy and his wife come to my house and Jimmy and Sonny had a fight and he beat up my husband, but Jimmy and a few of the boys must have jumped him on the site." She went on to say, "Look at the state he was left in, they must have all cut him to pieces," but Sonny couldn't back her up because he was asleep until the 22nd.

But before she got back to the hospital Sonny woke up and the police was there waiting. He wasted no time and gave a full statement, he said, "Me and Jimmy was fighting an arguing and Jimmy was really aggressive and he beat me up at my house, then he cut me up on the site." He made no mention of anyone else, but on the 23rd after a discussion between Sonny and his wife, I heard she supposedly told him that everyone was making a laugh of him by saying that Jimmy beat him easily. I think after hearing that from his woman Sonny felt ashamed because he had admitted to getting beat without realising what he had done so he tried to get his self out of it by changing his statement to the police. I think when she told him of her statement it put the idea in his head that if a gang of men beat him he wouldn't look as bad, so he went on to say to the police that me and my two sons jumped him, which completely contradicted his first statement, he said that me and my sons attacked him at his house, and then he said I hit him in the head with a hatchet, then after that he claimed to lose consciousness and then he said when he woke up, he drove down to my site where I was supposed to have cut him with a sword and then my boys were supposed to have jumped him as well. I was later told this back by someone that was standing by Sonny's bedside in the hospital. When he was giving his statement, the policeman asked him, "why did you go down to the site?" and Sonny said "to arrange a fair fight", and the policeman was supposed to have laughed at him and said jokingly, "three men attacked you with weapons at your house but you wanted a fair fight on their own ground?".

A while later the policeman asked Sonny, "Did you bring a knife to the site to stab Jimmy?"

"No," he said, he denied bringing a knife.

Anyway, on the 25th the police come onto the site looking for me and my two sons, so that afternoon me and the boys handed ourselves in. My son Willy had proof that he wasn't even there at the time, but regardless the three of us were still locked up. I was kept in for 15 hours and questioned multiple times and so were my son. I was charged with section 18 grievous bodily harm, maliciously wounding and attempted murder and even a section 45. My sons Willy and Thomas were charged with section 18 GBH and we were let out on conditional bail; we had a curfew from 11 p.m. till 8 a.m. and not to go into the area where Sonny's house was located. You see, at this time me and my sons never had no criminal record at all, which was very good for us. Anyway, I knew Sonny was a dirty bastard but I never knew he could stoop so low as to try and get two innocent children jail; he should have been a man and not brought them into our argument; even his wife made fake statements against my children and she knew that they were innocent, as was I.

Anyway, Sonny was about two weeks in hospital, and when he got out he was housebound for about six weeks, then he tried to play his games. Every day he would drive out on the roads looking for me and as soon as he'd seen me he would phone the police. There was days I never even left the site and he still got me locked up, by claiming I was somewhere where I wasn't. From June to October he had me arrested 33 times for threats to kill. One morning a CID came to me, he said, "If you get arrested one more time I'm putting you on remand."

I said to him, "Every time I drive out Sonny's getting me arrested even when I don't leave my home he still getting me arrested, what am I going to do?"

"I don't care," the policeman said, "but one more time and you are getting remanded."

I had to think outside the box so I contemplated on it for a bit of time and I came to the conclusion I had to put cameras on my plot. I put them everywhere, you could see my mobile, my shed, I was fully surveillance, and then I went and bought two for my car, one to look at the road and at the same time one to look at my face. At the time I didn't know nothing about the smartphones and technology because I'm old school, but I had to learn fast, especially having a dirty bastard like Sonny on my case. Anyway, a week went by and nothing happened. I thought someone must have tipped Sonny off that I had cameras on my plot, but then after about nine days I was sitting out drinking a cup of coffee on my table and chairs and out of the blue the police came in and arrested me. Apparently Sonny had claimed that I chased him down the Carmarthen Road, and threatened to cut him up. Well, Sonny had done exactly what I wanted him to do – when I was in the cell I was laughing, when I was interviewed the police asked me "where were you this morning at 9:30?" and I said "I was home sitting in my shed". They said, "have you got a witness?" and I said "I'll do one better than that, it's all on camera". The police didn't like it but they had to go and check my camera. When they looked at the video they could see me on it, eating my breakfast; the date and time was on it, which proved that Sonny was a liar. Surprisingly to me, the police were very upset but there was nothing they could do, they had to let me out with no charge; and then a week or so later I drove out and Sonny drives past me. I pulled straight into a garage and I waited. I knew the police were on the way, and when the police got there they said straight away "you are under arrest for threats to kill".

I said, "Hold it, officer, I've got everything recorded."

"Show me," he said.

So I played the video. You could see Sonny passing me and at the same time you could see my face and my movements. As soon as he had seen it the police officer said, "Well Sonny is caught straight out on a lie because he said you made a knife action across your throat."

I said, "Officer, only last week he had me arrested from my home and that also was proven to be a lie."

For a change he seemed to be a decent policeman, but even with the video evidence he still had to arrest me for an hour or so, just for the sergeant to look over the videos. As soon as I got out I gave this evidence to my solicitor. Meanwhile, we went to the magistrate court where I made the front page of the newspaper for coming into court with a pair of shorts on me; it was embarrassing, and the judge was not impressed, but I was never in court before and I didn't know not to wear them. We went to three crown courts and it was put back for a trial. Sonny tried every trick in the book to get me and my two children jail – he was going for psychiatric help, he was letting on he couldn't sleep and he was nervous to leave his house. I was in a dinner pub one night and I was chatting to a man – he was actually Sonny's psychiatrist, I couldn't believe my luck and he was talkative – he was telling me how him and the police were laughing at Sonny, he said he's meant to be this big hard man and when he comes in he is saying how nervous he is and how he needs a panic button in his house. The man was telling me this, I laughed but I couldn't believe what Sonny was doing to me and my children; he knew he could never beat me in any kind of a fight, so I believe that he told himself the only way I'm going to beat Jimmy is to get him jail.

Anyway, the trial was set for the 14th of January 2015, but in November 2014 my solicitor rang me to come in. When I got there he brought me into the office and sat me down, he said to me, "you've got to get your affairs in order".

I said, "Tell me straight how much jail is me and my children looking at?"

He said, "If you're found guilty, Jimmy, you're looking at 12 years and your son Willy is looking at six years. I might be able to get your son Thomas off with two years."

My wife broke down in tears. I tried to comfort her but what could I do? I wasn't bothered about myself, it was more my two children, so I said thank you to the solicitor and I headed home. A few days later I was chatting to one of my cousins and he asked me a question. He said, "Jimmy, would you be prepared to pay a few quid to Sonny to drop the charges?"

I said, "Maybe so, but it depends how much."

"Leave it with me," he said. That evening he come back to me and said that "Sonny will drop the charges if you give him a £100,000", so me and my wife had a chat about this and we decided it had to be done. I had a few quid about me and I asked my family to chip in the rest but £100,000 is a lot of money so it took me and my family a few days to get it together. It was arranged to hand the money to a cousin of mine to give to Sonny on the Saturday, then he was to drop the charges on the Monday, but a few days prior to this, being stupid, Sonny gave a few phone calls in saying that there was weed growing on my site. So on the Friday before the money drop the site was raided by the police. It was nothing to do with me but I was still very angry, so on principle I said to my wife "I'll do my jail, I'll never give him a penny". She was in a bit of a state, but I said I'll fight it out in court. I would say Sonny was kicking himself over phoning the police – he cost his own self £100,000 but Sonny never was the sharpest tool in the box haha.

Anyway, in December my son Thomas was fighting in Cardiff, I remember it was about 7 p.m. me and my wife were driving on the motorway and I got a phone call from the solicitor. He said, "Jimmy, brace yourself." I thought I was going on remand or something, but he said the CPS has dropped the case due to Sonny's conflicting statements and over him denying he brought a knife to the site which had his fingerprints and DNA all over it. You see, it's a man's word that puts you to jail and because Sonny had changed his statements and told so many lies and I recorded him lying about threats to kill his word meant nothing. Thank god justice prevailed. It turns out that not only could Sonny not beat me in a fair fight, a dirty fight or any other kind of a fight, he couldn't even get me jail, lol.

Anyway, the very next morning I sent word to Sonny that I wanted to fight him, I said, "you've got to fight, no way out of it". He sent word back, he said "you're getting no fight". Anyway, after a couple of weeks it got back to me that he was running around Swansea saying that I was a grass, just because of his stupidity and lying that his case against me and my children collapsed. I got very angry, I thought to myself the cheek of this man after nearly getting me and my children jail and even saying that there was weed growing on my site – if that's not grassing I don't know what is. Anyway, being a proper man and a man that's got pride in my reputation, I decided to put a YouTube video up to clear my name. My father advised me not to do it because he calls YouTube and Facebook the devil's playground and I agree, he was 100% right, because when you put a video up it's a vicious cycle because when they put a video back to you, you've got to put more up and so on and so forth, which is bad, especially when you're dealing with a vile person like Sonny, who took it to a different level, the lies, scandal and filthy talk he came out with was scandalous. You see, my grandfather always reared his sons with a certain manner which my father passed to his sons, and it was to have a bit of pride and respect, but at this point Sonny had lost all that in himself and in his name; but in truth I didn't care about the rubbish and lies Sonny was coming out with, all I wanted was a fight. I was pushing him hard to come out to me, because the way I saw it, he had to be punished for what he had done, especially to my children, but he would not fight.

Anyway, 2015 was a war of YouTubes, but I had to be very careful what I was saying on the videos because Sonny was reporting everything to the police, and at the time I was afraid of bringing the case back up. But he'd done a stupid thing when he was arguing with me, he had the cheek to bring my brother Michael's name into his mouth. This infuriated Michael so he asked me could he fight Sonny first, and I said "Michael, he won't fight, I'm literally begging him to fight me, but you can try". So he told Sonny straight that he wanted to fight him, Michael gave Sonny eight weeks to get ready. Meanwhile, my father was running a site in Merthyr Tydfil as the warden, he was aware of Sonny's carry on, on the old videos, but my father is old fashioned – you see, as far as my father was concerned, if two men have an argument, get out and fight and that's the end of it; but Sonny and his rats had different plans.

Anyway, at the time my brothers Martin, Peter, and Bucky were staying on the site with my father. To get to the point, a few of the gypsy people were growing a bit of weed for a smoke, but listen, what a man does on his own plot is his own business, but Sonny and his rats didn't see it like that, all Sonny and his rats saw was an opportunity to get my father and brothers jail, so they put in over 100 phone calls saying that my father was the kingpin of a drugs ring. It was a load of rubbish but nevertheless my father and my brothers got locked up for conspiracy to grow weed, just because my father was the warden, it was ridiculous. Anyway after a few days locked up everyone was expecting them to get out on bail, but when they were brought out to court my father and brothers were put on six months remand, it was unbelievable; and when my father and the boys were in jail Sonny was right on me and Michael and my sons' case, we could not drive out on the road without getting pulled up for suspicion of having weapons in our motors – my son Thomas was pulled up six times in one day. At this point Sonny and his rats were full-blown police informants, Sonny had lost all honour in himself, he was and is a disgrace; all he was good for was making YouTube videos, calling names, scandalising women and children and talking about dead people, and when I made a video back to try and have my say he would report it to the police and get it taken down, he was a show.

Anyway, his eight weeks was up, so me and Michael went out to Briton Ferry on the date that was given to Sonny for the fight, but after numerous phone calls Sonny would not answer his phones and he wouldn't turn up, but he did send police to the location in his stead. At this point Sonny was only trying to get us all jail, the way he was carrying on even his own family was getting ashamed of him. At the time, they were all telling me, "I don't understand why Sonny won't come out and fight." I laughed and said, "it's because he is a coward". They held their heads down in shame.

Anyway, a few months later my father and brothers were found not guilty which was a blow to Sonny and his rats, they had failed again, thank God. Not long after there was a funeral but I stayed out of the way for the sakes of respect; however, Sonny had other ideas. He sent word down to me to come down to the Dylan Thomas to fight. I said, "No problem, I'll be down right now", but when I drove in Sonny was nowhere to be seen, the only people there were from the funeral, so I felt a bit ashamed and I drove out of the car park, and as I did I thought to myself Sonny was just a low life tramp. You see, normally I would just drive straight to Sonny's house and break his face in, but because he had me out on such bad charges, I had to be careful not to bring the case back up and that is why I had to get him to admit on a tape that he wanted to fight, because at the time he was playing the victim to the police.

Anyway, I made my way home from the Dylan Thomas, and when I got back to the site, my wife said, "Why don't we go and get a takeaway?" I said "that will do", so I drove back up to Morriston. My wife went in to get things for the night and some food. I was sitting in my car minding my own business when Sonny tried to get me off-guard, there was Sonny and three of his rats, or donkeys as I would call them. Sonny pulled up fast in his car and he runs across the road at me, I glimpsed him out of the corner of my eye, and thank God I reacted quickly. I managed to jump out of my car and as he ran towards me I hit him a glancing right hand, and then I spun him to the ground. I was going to kick the face off him but then I saw one of the other men with a knife, I knew their game. I was gonna throw caution to the wind but just as I was going to get stuck in one of them started shouting "get the police". In truth only for the law I would have picked a weapon and hurt them very badly, but I knew Sonny was trying to get me jail by any means, so I had to try and stay a step ahead of him. As soon as I left Morriston Sonny phoned the police, but when the police came and arrested me they started looking over the video evidence, so ironically, they also arrested Sonny and his rats, and we were all charged with a section 5 affray fighting in public.

After this court case I had had enough so I went to a family member belonging to Sonny and I put it right on his toes. I said, "Sonny has got to fight, he's gone too far, so he's as well to come out to me because it's going to get very bad if he don't."

"Ok," he said, "I will talk to him."

I was sick of Sonny and his dirty mouth up and down the comments and videos, so I went on the bear, all over the Christmas. I thought if I'm going to go to jail for him I'm as well enjoying my Christmas. In truth I didn't think that Sonny would actually fight, I thought I would have to go to him and break him up, but before I could do anything he finally manned up. In February of 2016 Sonny put a video up claiming he wanted to fight. This was great news for me. I put a reply video up and accepted the fight, I never set no date because I always like to go to the gym and see how much time I need to get fighting fit. Being gym fit is one thing but when it comes to fighting it's a complete different ball game, but all of that don't make any difference because the rules in bare-knuckle dictate that when a man challenges you, you have the right to set the date and time and even the location.

Anyway, after a couple of weeks when I was ready I gave Sonny his date the 16th of April. Celebrity Paddy Doherty and Joe McAllister were the fair play men, they were selected to sort out the fight but all of the logistics meant nothing to me, all I wanted to do was to knock

Sonny out on a video. But for the full length of time that I was pushing Sonny for a fight he was in the gym training flat out, fair play to him because I should have been doing the same thing, but in all fairness three months' training will get any man fit. Even so, he played me well, he had me fooled that he wasn't going to fight, but because he was ready he had plenty of time to play mind games and to try and put me off my game plan, by scandalising women and children and talking about dead people; but I am a very focused man when it comes to gym training, nothing distracts me. But little did he know what he was doing was working to my advantage, I began playing the mind games back to Sonny. For instance, I was jogging one morning and from the distance I saw one of his family members. I let on not to see them, I pretended to stop and let on to be out of breath. This was brought back to Sonny – I know this because he mentioned it to a cousin of mine, and when it was said back to me I laughed to myself, but I knew it made Sonny feel confident and when a man feels like that he thinks he doesn't have to do that extra mile on the road or that extra half hour in the gym. But that was his mistake because on the morning of the fight my fitness was 100-percent, I could have sprinted ten miles or easily fought for two hours and this was all thanks to my son Willy as my main trainer and my brother Michael and my son Thomas, they pushed me hard and got me into great shape.

Anyway, the day before the fight, me, my brother Michael and my boys, drove to Queensferry, we got a hotel where we met up with Danny and Joe McAllister. That night we had a very good laugh with the boys, but on the morning of the fight it was all business, I was fully focused and 100-percent confident. At about 11am Paddy Doherty phoned me, he said, "Jimmy, I can't get Sonny on the phone, it's switched off."

I cracked a joke and said to Paddy I had a feeling he wasn't going to turn up. He started laughing, but then I got serious and said, "All jokes aside, Paddy the fight is arranged for 12:00 midday, if he's not there by 12 he loses his fight. I'm claiming victory." I put down the phone, within

20 minutes Paddy rings me back. "I've just got a hold of him, fight's on for 12."

I said, "That will do, Paddy, I'll be there."

I knew Sonny wanted me to wait around half the day to try and tire me. I laughed to myself, because at this point I knew all Sonny's old tricks and I was too wise to him. Anyway, me and Joe and his father Danny and my son Willy, went to the fight. My son Thomas and my brother Michael went with the rest

Me and Sonny fighting

of the lads and waited in the pub. I was feeling supremely confident, I was willing to die on that day before I would let Sonny beat me. Anyway, Sonny walks into the yard and we come face-to-face; the fight kicks off. I tried to line him up for a right hand but when I threw it I was awkward and off balance and he caught me an awkward punch and dropped me. In truth this just woke me up, I jumped up and I got back into him, I threw a right hook and connected him on the temple which dropped

him on his ass; he jumped back up. I threw a straight right cross and dropped him again. He gets back up, I runs back in and hits him a right uppercut and a right hook and knocked him out.

Paddy Doherty and Joe McAllister stopped the fight because Sonny could not continue. He later got on a video, sitting on a pool table with Paddy, and admitted he lost his fight. He said, "The better man won on the day and I wish you luck with the title." I thought this is out of character for Sonny, but even I had to admit and say to the boys fair play to him for doing that, but the minute he got out from Paddy Doherty, his true colours showed through. You see, by trying to claim he did not lose the fight he made an absolute fool of himself. I think if he would have left it at the pool table video he would have had a lot more respect, but the simpleton had his leg on the dash of a car crying like a child, that his leg was broken, but at the end of the day he never came with a broken leg, the truth is no matter what excuse he comes up with it made no difference because I finally had a video of me beating him and even then he was still trying to deny he lost. But the more he cried about his leg all he did was got me the nickname the legbreaker. At the time I wasn't really into the nicknames but I know by calling myself the legbreaker, it got on Sonny's nerves so that is why I took the name, just to piss him off lol.

Anyway, when me and the boys got back to Swansea we went to the pub to celebrate our victory over Sonny. We were all laughing about the names like the legbreaker and jawbreaker, and then out of the blue my

brother Bucky looked up and said we should be known as the bone breakers. I looked up laughing. I said, "That will do, brother, I christen you the skull cracker." He didn't like that name, but we had a good night and a good laugh.

Meanwhile, Sonny made more videos complaining that he never lost the fight, so out of honour's sake Paddy Doherty and Joe McAllister made a couple of videos, to clarify that I won my fight and Sonny had lost. Sonny actually made his wife phone Paddy and she had the cheek to ask him to make a video saying that Sonny won the fight. The man obviously started laughing at her, he said, "My word stands, Sonny lost his fight, end of story." Sonny's wife was that upset that he lost, she actually left him for six or seven months – yes they separated over the fight!

Anyway, Sonny carried on with his videos. He upset me a few times but as far as I was concerned I had nothing to prove, but even so I still put it on a tape that if he wants to fight it's not a problem, I will oblige him. But in fairness, how many times do you have to beat one man? You see, he would always come up with an excuse no matter how many times I beat him, but at the end of the day the whole reason for this fight was to punish him for telling lies on my two innocent children, and as far as I was concerned he was punished, so I tried to put it all behind me and move on with my life.

CHAPTER 14

ANYWAY, MOVING FORWARD: within a month of each other my sons Willy and Thomas got married. Everything was going great for me, but in September of 2016 my father got bad news – his sister Violet had just passed away, she was only 59 years old, she was known as the queen of the travellers, a lovely woman, she reared a respectable family. My aunt Violet was a good person, she would always give you a kind word, she was the matriarch of the Gilheaney family. Me and my brothers and my father went back to Ireland to her funeral to pay our respects. We were in the church from about 8 in the morning till about 4 in the afternoon. My cousin Alec Crumlish and his family gave us the best of welcome and respect, we were shaking hands and just ready to go when at the last minute Sonny walked in with a Del boy coat on him. I've got to be truthful, I was going to kick his brains in, but out of respect for my aunt Violet and my father I held back. Sonny held his head down and wouldn't look none of us in the eye; he was no more than 20 minutes in the graveyard and he left, so we thought nothing of it. But a few days later he put a YouTube video up, giving his usual cheek and saying that he rode us out of the graveyard. He obviously didn't realise that there were 200 people in the graveyard looking at him holding his head down, but the facts don't mean much to Sonny, he lives in his own little world. Regardless of that though, he still upset me, so I replied immediately and told him to get straight to Swansea for an immediate fight. He went quiet and wouldn't take the fight, and after a few days I realised he was full of hot air so I couldn't be bothered with him, I had better things happening in my life.

Anyway, in 2017 my first grandchild was born, baby Nikisha, my son Willy's daughter, things couldn't be better. Six days a week me and my sons were working flat out, we were in the gym four days a week, my life was coming back on track nicely, it was a hard couple of years: me and my children nearly going to jail, a rat like Sonny on the internet giving cheek and trying to take my reputation; it was a relief to have it all behind me. So I said to my wife, "No matter how many videos Sonny makes I'm going to try and blank him."

Anyway, moving forward, I remember at the time my brother Bucky's son was fighting so me and my brother Michael decided to go and support him. When we got to the bar in the boxing show me and Michael looked at one another and looked back at Bucky. I said jokingly, "who's buying the first pint", Bucky laughed and said, "get out your money, boys". Needless to say it was left to me to buy the first round, the three of us brothers got well drunk, we had the best time. Bucky's son won his fight and we had a very good laugh. The next day I got up with a bad hangover. I decided to focus on my four sons and get them back into serious boxing. My two youngest sons Pio and Jimmy started doing very well, they were winning a good few fights, my older sons Willy and Thomas were getting ready to go pro, but I was advising them to hold back for at least a couple of years or until they matured into fully grown men. They agreed.

Anyway, on another note in June of 2017 I got news that Sonny was bullying a couple of my cousins at a funeral and they cut him up with a machete. This had nothing to do with me, but he put up more YouTube videos arguing with my cousins and he mentioned my name, so in July I put it to him to come and sort this out once and for all, but instead of coming to fight he was trying to get other men to fight me. In truth he was afraid to face me himself, but listen, I didn't care who he got for me because Sonny or any man that stepped in for him would never beat me because I was prepared to die before I would let them get the best of me. But before any of this could happen in August of 2017 Sonny went bullying an old woman and broke her mobile home up, and on the same night a young lad by the name of Will Jones took him out and gave him a beating which was humiliating because the boy was half his size. Fair enough, Sonny was drunk and he had an injury to his hand, but he still looked bad. The way I'd seen it, at this point he couldn't be taken seriously, he had degraded to a level which my little girl could beat, so I decided to put Sonny behind me and to try and move on.

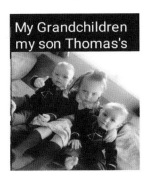

My Grandchildren my son Thomas's

Anyway, in October 2017, my second grandchild was born, Natalia, my son Thomas's daughter, and in November my daughter Thoots got married. We had a very good night, my brother Michael and my brother Bucky and all the family danced, laughed and joked all night, it was one of the best nights I've had in years and everyone that attended said the same thing, the atmosphere was fantastic. After my daughter's wedding I was looking forward to having a nice quiet family Christmas, but on the 21st of December my brother Michael booked into a holiday park in Porthcawl with one of my cousins. The day before Christmas Eve Michael went into the pub on the site, and started drinking. He drank through the day, into the evening. At around 11 that night a fellow by the name of young Joe Joyce walked into the pub sober. I knew this because he phoned me when he was there, he wanted to meet up on Christmas Day to get a photo with me. I started laughing, I said, "No problem, Joe, I'll have a photo with you", I said, "I'll see you Christmas morning." Joe laughed and joked and said, "Ok, Jimmy." Joe gave the phone back to Michael, I said, "Goodnight, brother, I'll see you tomorrow." At the time Michael was well drunk. Anyway, Joe had four other men with him, one of the men was called Mushy Joyce. Michael and Joe carried on drinking in the pub till about two in the morning then they decided to take a carry out back to Joe's mobile home. After getting there a persuading match took place, Joe was saying how his father was the king of the travellers, and Michael looked up. "Well, if your father is the king, so is mine." Because of this an argument kicked off. You see, two men game for a fight shouldn't drink together because at the end of the night it's a guaranteed argument. Anyway, without going into too much detail – because at the end of the day I wasn't there – but that night Michael and Joe would both claim victory. Anyway, the next morning Davy Joyce rang me up to ask me what happened, he talked with respect and actually came across sensible. He was worried about his brother, he sounded very concerned, so listen, I spoke sensible back to the man. Anyway, after speaking to Davy I went out and spoke to Michael. He said, "After Christmas I will arrange a fair fight." I said, "That will do, brother." Shortly after the holidays Michael was in the process of arranging a fair fight, and just as Michael was trying to get the fight on, when out of nowhere young Joe challenged me, which was alright, but how could I step on my brother's toes? At the end of the day Michael wanted to fight Joe first, but listen, I had no problem at all fighting Joe, but before I even decided to take the fight or not, out of the blue Davy Joyce also challenged me. Anyway, listen, me and my brother Michael were as game as two Yankee cocks to get those fights on, but just as it was progressing big Joe Joyce put a video up to my father explaining his case that he didn't want his sons fighting us and when my father had seen the video, he thought the man talked since, so my father sat us down and explained the case to us, and listen, we don't go against our father – what he says goes – but in truth I think the Joyce brothers hold the same respect for their father as we do for ours, and because of that the fights were left at a drunken argument and as far as we were concerned that was that. Anyway, after the Joyce argument I decided to get back to a normal way of life if there is such a thing for a traveller. At this point my brothers were doing very well buying and selling scrap cars, my brother Bucky was especially doing very well he was working from dusk till dawn. On the 29th of January 2018 he had a lorry full of aluminium wheels, that he'd taken off the old scrap cars that he was collecting. He started cutting the tyres off the rims with a disc cutter, and as a result the smoke was going everywhere from the rubber tyres. Anyway, he worked all day on the 29th and on the 30th he worked into the evening, he finished and loaded up his pickup and strapped the rims down ready to weigh in to the scrapyard the next morning. Anyway, after work he went out laughing and joking with my brother Michael. Michael had broken his ankle while he was jogging and like brothers do Bucky was making a laugh of him. Anyway, after having a bit of fun Bucky and Michael went in chatting to my mother and father, my brother Bucky got into a bit of a kink over Michael's leg, they all had a good laugh. When Bucky went back over to his own place he stood at his fence and said goodnight to my brother Michael, he went into watch his programmes that he was into, I think it was the Game of Thrones. Anyway, he had himself some snacks and a bowl of ice cream, and then he decided to go to bed. It was a very windy night and it was raining from the heavens; my brother Bucky was restless, he thought he could hear someone trying to steal his aluminium rims. He got up to check what was going on and when he looked he could see nothing was wrong but while he was up he decided to go to the toilet. As he walked out of his shed he collapsed on his plot, and after a few minutes his wife noticed that he did not come back in. When she walked out she saw him on the ground, she started shouting and roaring which alerted everyone on the site. My brother was lying there with the rain beating off him, and as the ambulance was on its way my brother Michael was trying to help him. When the crew got there they were giving him CPR and pumping his chest in front of my mother and father. My brother was lying on the concrete in the rain, freezing cold and soaking wet, my old mother and father had to stand anxiously looking at the paramedics trying to save their son's life. My mother was panicking and crying, begging God not to take her child, my father was trying to comfort her, but he was panicking himself. The crew finally lifted my brother into the ambulance, they rushed him to the hospital. While my brother Michael was following the ambulance, he phoned me. I thought it was a late phone call so I looked at the time; it was three in the morning. He said to me, "You've got to get to Bridgend hospital straight away," he said, "I think our Bucky is dead." He was panicking and crying.

At this point I was in shock, I couldn't believe what I was hearing. I said, "Calm down, our Michael, and tell me what's going on."

He said, "I'm following the ambulance to the hospital, Bucky's in the ambulance and he's not breathing."

I said, "I'm on my way, I'll be there as fast as my car can bring me." I jumped up and got into my car. From Swansea to Bridgend is about 20 miles and I got there in about nine and a half minutes which will tell you the speed I was doing, but when I got there everyone was panicking and crying, I tried to make sense of what was happening, I tried to talk to a doctor, but all I could find was a nurse. She told me that they were doing everything they could to try and save his life. After about 30 minutes the doctor came out and said that my brother's heart had stopped, but they managed to get back a bit of a heartbeat. My old mother broke down in tears, she sobbed like a baby and my father begged God to leave him his son, the tears were pouring down his old face. I've never seen my father cry like that before, the only way I can describe how I felt at that time it was like I was falling off a cliff and there was nothing I could do, that's how I felt. Everyone was crying. The doctor had told us if his heart stops again they're not going to resuscitate him; everyone was in shock, it was unbelievable. Anyway, at about six in the morning the doctor came out to my father, put his hand on his shoulder, and told him, "we did everything we could but your son has died, I'm so sorry," the doctor said. My father broke down in tears, my mother was hysterical, my brothers and sisters did not know what to do with themselves. I was in shock because only for a bit of asthma Bucky was perfectly healthy, he was fit and strong anyway. The next few days were a blur, at the time nothing felt real. After about a week everyone was saying to me, "Why don't you go and see your brother?" I was tossing with the idea, I didn't want to see my brother like that, but I knew if I didn't say goodbye I would never get the chance again, so I decided to go into the funeral home to see my brother. It was the worst thing I ever did; I can't explain the feeling that come over me, I felt like I was going to suffocate, I touched his hair and said goodbye but I panicked and left the funeral home. That memory will haunt me forever, I had seen people like this before but when it's your own close family it's a complete different thing, it's something I will never do again if I can help it. I think it's better to remember your loved ones the way they were. Anyway, in the days leading up to the funeral people were coming to pay their respects and all the family were so grateful. The night before the funeral me and my brothers, Martin and Michael and my brother-in-law William made a pact to grow a beard out for one year for respect of my brother Bucky. Now that doesn't sound hard to do, but believe me it was hard; all of us were so lost, but what else could we do? The next day my brother Bucky was laid to rest, he had a very good send off, hundreds of people came to show their respect, for which we were very grateful. When he died my brother was only 35 years old, he left five young children. To this day we don't know how he died, the doctors

HUNDREDS have turned out for the funeral of a scrap dealer dad-of-five whose sudden death shocked the traveller community

He was a very loving, very caring family man." Floral tributes left for Gilheaney included boxes of Malteasers, Flakes and a fork-lift truck.

suggested that he might've had heart arrhythmia, but in truth I don't think we will ever know what happened to him. Some of my family thought the smoke of the tyres might have had something to do with it because he had asthma. It's just an awful thing for someone so young and strong to lose his life without an answer, but one thing for sure his loss has devastated my family and we will never be the same again. This book is dedicated to my brother, to his memory, until we meet again – he will be loved and missed forever. My brother's name was Steven Francis Gilheaney – he got the nickname Bucky from my aunt Mary, she used to say to him "come to me, my chicken", and after a while the name chicken stuck to him, but us as children, every time he upset us we kept waving our arms and saying to him, buk, buk, buk, like a chicken. In time the name evolved to Bucky and it stuck on him. Anyway, the next couple of months was really hard, especially for my mother and father, we were all trying to comfort them the best way that we could but what can you honestly say to someone who has lost a young man of 35 years old? No parent should have to go through that. 2018 was proving to be a very bad year, and not only for my family because on the 5th of May I was sitting out on my table and chairs drinking a cup of coffee when I got a phone call from a nephew of mine, he tells me that my wife's brother, Parr, had fallen off a ladder and banged his head. I said, "is he alright?" and he told me that Parr was sitting up in the ambulance and he gave the paramedic his telephone number but then he blanked out and he was very bad in hospital. I jumped up and sorted the children out, got Bridget and shot straight through to Nottingham hospital. When we got there there was a lot of screaming and crying; I couldn't work out what was happening but when I eventually got a doctor, she explained to me that when Parr fell off the ladder and banged his head, a blood clot had formed at the back of his skull, and it busted through his brain; there was no hope for him at all, and they would have to turn off the machines. My wife Bridget was absolutely devastated, as was I, life can be very cruel. Parr died the next day, he was only 46 years old, he fell no more than five foot. Parr's two sons Billy and Patrick gave him a very good send off, Parr was always into old-time motors and they got an old shape transit pickup to carry him to the graveyard, he would have been proud of his sons for that. Parr was laid to rest with his brother Thomas and alongside his mother and father in Doncaster.

The day after the funeral I made my way back to Swansea. I remember that year it was very hot and me and the boys had long beards that we were growing out for my brother Bucky, but after seven months it was anguish, I never wanted to shave so much in my life, but I had to carry on for respect. And on top of everything that was going on in August of 2018 out of the blue Sonny started messaging and calling names, he told my brother Michael that he had climbed over the back fence of my brother Bucky's plot, and he said he hit Bucky with a hammer in the head and that is the reason that Bucky died. This infuriated the whole family. I told Sonny on a voice note to get straight down for a fight, so I could break him up, even though at this point he wasn't worth my time. He completely blanked me and he carried on giving cheek and sending messages like a child to my brother Bucky's wife and his boys. Me and Michael were begging him for a fight but he was just making a laugh, so I said to the boys, "When we see him in the right place we'll give him a beating, other than that, boys, he's only a fool, he's just provoking us to get one of us jail." I also told the boys we had to think of our parents, because at the end of the day my poor old mother and father had more on their mind than watching their sons having an argument or going to jail for a washed-up has-been of a man.

So I decided to turn my attention to my own little family. In October of that year my third granddaughter was born, my daughter Thoots' little girl Olivia, she has bright red hair just like her granny Bridget, which I thought was very cute. Anyway, in November me and my brother Michael decided to do a half marathon in memory of my brother Bucky, it wasn't really hard for us because we keep in half decent shape all year round, but I remember running it and thinking of my brother Bucky sitting in a pub laughing at me. His words would be "what are you doing running, mong boy, sit back and have a pint". As I was running one second I was laughing to myself and in the next I was crying, it was very emotional. Me and Michael finished it in good time, but my big toenail fell off a few days later – it must have been the hills up and down, or maybe Bucky having a joke with me. Anyway what was to happen next got me thinking of what an old woman once told me, she said the man with the slippers never sleeps. I didn't know at the time what she meant but I've learnt that she meant God pays his debts without money. Either way karma is a bitch because at the end of November Sonny's son was arguing with a cousin of mine, the boy was only 16 and he beat Sonny's son in a fair fight but Sonny's boy picked a pick handle and tried to attack my cousin. Allegedly Sonny's boy got cut down the face, so Sonny went and run the 16-year old boy over with his car. Sonny was put on remand because of this and in January 2019 he got 32 months in jail. I wouldn't wish it on no one but because of it me and my family had a bit of time to grieve, because no doubt the way we were feeling either me or one of my brothers would have done jail for Sonny, so it was for the best.

Anyway, when someone dies in the travelling community we like to hold a blessing, and what that means is we get a priest to bless the headstone every year, it's just our way to show respect and to keep the memory of them alive for the younger generation. Anyway at the end of January 2019 we were due to hold a big blessing for my brother Bucky, but due to a technicality his headstone was not ready in time so we had to put the blessing back to the 17th of February which was the day he was buried. Anyway, hundreds of people came to my brother's blessing to show their respect. At the time me and my family were very proud of the love that was there for my brother. Anyway the next morning while

Me and my brothers and sisters

I was having a laugh with my grandchildren, I shaved off the beard that I grew out as a sign of respect for my brother – it was a good thing to do but it was very hard; there were days I could have ripped it off my face. I think any man that has attempted to grow a big beard will know what I'm on about. Anyway, when the beard was off and everything was over I decided to sort out some unfinished business with a couple of Sonny's rats. Anyway, as I was figuring out the best way to go about it, my father told me, he said, "Son, watch what you're doing with those people because they are jail waiting to happen." My father was right in what he was saying and at the end of the day I didn't want to go to jail for a couple of donkeys, which could have easily happened because those fellas got me and my sons arrested no end of times, so I had to box clever. I thought about it for a bit and I decided to push them to have a fair fight. I told them, "I'll have youse one at a time or the two of youse together whichever way youse want it." They obviously had a chat between themselves and they sent out the best they had, but on the morning that I was going to go out and give him a couple of slaps, my wife said be careful because if you hurt them they will get you jail, and she made me promise her not to open up properly on him. She said, "Only do enough for him to quit." I said, "I will try." Now the fellow wasn't a fighting man, far from it, but when you hit with the power that I have, you've got to be careful because if a man's neck is not trained up there is a possibility if you swing full blast you could hurt them, so when

I took him out I only used one hand and I only threw three punches and after 20 seconds, he quit. But to be truthful at one point I almost lost my temper and I was going to rip into him properly, but I remembered I gave my wife my word and because he come out like a man, I had to hold respect, it was a thing of nothing but I just put a family feud to bed, so as long as they stayed out of me and my family's way that was the end of it as far as I was concerned.

CHAPTER 15

ANYWAY, MOVING FORWARD, 2019 was a good year. I had a great summer. I genuinely put everything behind me and moved on with my life. In November of that year my sons Pio and Jimmy were fighting. I hadn't seen them box in a while but on the night I was very impressed, Pio stopped his boy in the first round and Jimmy beat his boy on points, I was very proud. In December my son Thomas was preparing to go pro, but before he did he decided to have one last amateur fight. Anyway the boy he boxed had 108 fights, and he even had a 10 kilo weight advantage, but fair play to my Thomas he got stuck straight into him, but I won't lie it was a hell of a fight, it was literally shot for shot for three rounds. No doubt about it, the boy was a strong lad, but they don't call my Thomas the tank for nothing; he bit down on his gum shield and beat the boy convincingly. Thomas went into that fight as a boy and he walked out as a man. That night when I'd seen his determination, I knew Thomas was capable of being a world champion.

Anyway, moving forward, I had a quiet family Christmas, and like everyone else I had big plans for the new year but 2020 had its own plans lol. Now what can I say about this year? Well, in January there was threats of World War 3, in February there were three storms that hit the UK, one after the other, and in March the coronavirus hit. I remember thinking that it could be the end of the world lol. Anyway, when the coronavirus hit the UK the full country went into lockdown. I've never seen nothing like it in my life, it was literally like a film, but after the initial shock I realised it was not as bad as the news was making it out and in truth I actually enjoyed the rest of the year. I had plenty of quality time with the family and I even had three extra grandchildren born in that year – my first grandson Thomas and two more granddaughters Mia and Renesmee. Needless to say they kept me busy lol.

Anyway, in March 2021 my cousin Sammy lee was getting married and everywhere was locked down so he asked me was it ok to put a marquee in the middle of the site for his reception. I said, "No problem, cousin, carry on." The tent was massive, and it was a good job because there was a good 250 people in attendance. Anyway, it was a great wedding, everyone was enjoying themselves, well until the end of the night when this Evans man started at my son Willy – the fool chucked a piece of chicken at my son. Willy thought he was having a laugh so he said, "Are you ok, mate?" The Evans man threw two punches at him. Willy steps to the side and hit him a sharp one-two and dropped him. The Evans man was trying to bite Willy's leg so out of instinct he

Me bridgie and our daughters

leaned down and ripped the Evans man's ear off and hit him two more shots and knocked him out cold. By this time everyone had intervened and pulled my son Willy back. I didn't quite know what was going on so I ran over to my son and when he explain to me what the Evans man had done I saw red, I thought the cheek of him to do that on a Gilheany man's ground. It didn't occur to me that my son Willy had just slaughtered him in seconds, but in fairness I was well drunk. Anyway, I ran after the man and no exaggeration a good 30 people came out of nowhere and jumped on me. They were trying to hold me back but because I was drunk I couldn't be reasoned with, I went mental and mowed them down. The boys told me afterwards that it looked like a bowling ball smashing through pins lol. Anyway, one man hit off the front tow bar of a trailer and he was nearly killed lol, but by the time I got out to the road the Evans man had got away. On his escape up the lane he broke up six or seven cars, it was obviously due to panic but the truth is I was glad he got away because my son Willy beat him in seconds so there was no need for me to intervene. Anyway, the next morning I managed to get the Evans man on the phone, my son Willy wanted to take him out to give him a hiding but after a bit of deliberation the man apologised so I told my son to leave it as a drunken argument and after a little bit of persuading he agreed with me, so as far as we were concerned that was that.

Anyway, moving forward, in January 2022 I got the news that my great-uncle Willy, my grandfather's youngest brother, had passed away, he was 82 years old. I know he had had a good long life but it was still a sad time for all the family because he was well liked and well respected by everyone and also he was the last of the old breed of the Gilheaneys which was kinda bringing an end to a big chapter in the family. Anyway, his funeral was to be held in Morriston cemetery but as usual word was coming back to me and my family that Sonny wanted to fight. Listen, when I heard it I laughed because as far as I'm concerned Sonny is a washed up fighter, but regardless of that we still didn't want trouble at the old man's funeral so my brother Michael put a video up and he gave Sonny the option to fight me or Michael before the funeral, but Sonny never replied and on the day of the funeral he never showed up – which was for the best because my uncle Willy had a very good send off with no trouble and everyone that attended showed the height of respect and I was glad because I had good time for my uncle Willy, he was a nice old man and he will be missed.

Anyway, after the funeral I vowed to wash my hands of Sonny. I even said to the lads when I see him if he turns his head from me first then I will turn mine from him because at the end of the day I have nothing more to prove with Sonny, but if it's any consolation to him I don't claim to be the king or the boss; but the truth is that I am a hard fight for anyone and if Sonny admits it to himself I was always the better man. Listen, I don't like Sonny but I will tell the truth: in his day he could have a fight, he was just not on my level. Listen, if Sonny realised to himself that there's no shame at all in losing to a man like me I think he could finally move on with his life, because like I said I'm capable of beating anyone and like it or not I'm up there with the very best of men, but like in any family argument there just comes a time when you've got to say enough is enough, so on that note, Sonny, I say to you goodbye.

Anyway, moving forward a couple of months later I was in a dinner pub having a few beers with my wife, and when I looked up I saw my uncle Peter walking in. The man looked a bit worried but regardless we had a good night and a good laugh, we shook hands, hugged one another and left the pub. As it does, the year went quick and Christmas came around so me and my brothers Martin and Michael and my son Thomas all decided to drive to Spain. We all had a very good time and a wonderful family Christmas; anyway, on the way home I stopped off in Lourdes and got all my family blessed, it was a beautiful place and we all really enjoyed it. Anyway when I got home life was going on as normal but in January I got the news that my uncle Peter had passed away, he was only 72. You see, unbeknownst to me, the day I met him in the pub he had received bad news and he was only given months to live, it was a crying sin because my uncle Peter was a gentleman and was well respected and liked through the whole country. His son Peter and his

Me and my uncle Peter

wife Margaret and all his daughters gave him a very good send off; he was buried in Morriston not far from my brother Bucky. Sonny showed up at the funeral but he turned his head so I turned mine and there was no trouble, thank God.

Anyway, as I look back at my life I have to ask myself a question: have I made mistakes? – yes I have; am I perfect? – no, I am not. But the truth is, is that no one is perfect and we all make mistakes, we would not be human if we didn't, but would I change anything? I don't think I would because I have learnt that everything you do through your life, whether it be good or bad, it all makes you into the person you are now, and the truth is after a lot of ups and downs in my life I am finally happy with who I am. I am a family man, I have nine healthy, beautiful grandchildren, five girls and four boys, all my family are healthy and well, I am truly a blessed man. I have a beautiful wife that I love from the bottom of my heart and she truly is my best friend, she has been there for me through thick and thin and I would be lost without her, she is my rock. Anyway, I would just like to say thanks to everyone that read this book, I hope you enjoyed it and I wish everyone that read it the very best in your life. Big love and respect from Jimmy Gilheaney and all of my family, good luck and God bless and to be continued.

Me and my wife Bridget

Printed in Great Britain
by Amazon

42757974R00073